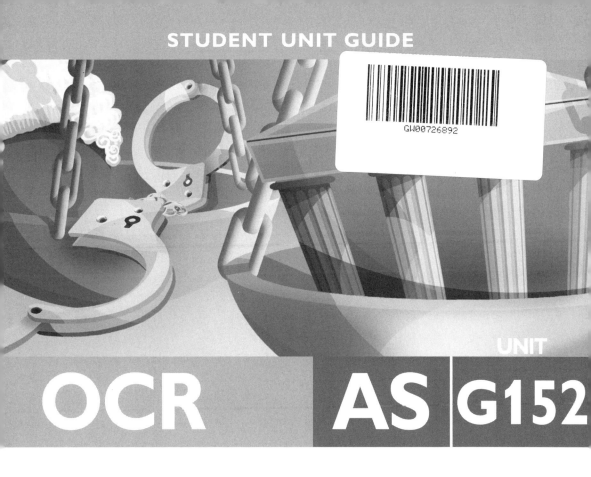

OCR **AS** UNIT **G152**

Law

Sources of Law

Chris Turner and Leon Riley

Philip Allan Updates, an imprint of Hodder Education, an Hachette UK Company, Market Place, Deddington, Oxfordshire OX15 0SE

Orders
Bookpoint Ltd, 130 Milton Park, Abingdon, Oxfordshire OX14 4SB
tel: 01235 827720
fax: 01235 400454
e-mail: uk.orders@bookpoint.co.uk
Lines are open 9.00 a.m.–5.00 p.m., Monday to Saturday, with a 24-hour message answering service. You can also order through the Philip Allan Updates website: www.philipallan.co.uk

© Philip Allan Updates 2009

ISBN 978-1-84489-017-0

First printed 2009
Impression number 5 4 3 2 1
Year 2013 2012 2011 2010 2009

This guide has been written specifically to support students preparing for the OCR AS Law Unit G152 examination. The content has been neither approved nor endorsed by OCR and remains the sole responsibility of the authors.

Typeset by Phoenix Photosetting, Chatham, Kent
Printed by MPG Books, Bodmin

Hachette UK's policy is to use papers that are natural, renewable and recyclable products and made from wood grown in sustainable forests. The logging and manufacturing processes are expected to conform to the environmental regulations of the country of origin.

Contents

Introduction

■ ■ ■

Content Guidance

■ ■ ■

Questions and Answers

Introduction

About this guide

This study guide is written for students following the OCR AS Law course and covers the specification content for **Unit G152: Sources of Law**. The selection of topics in this module is designed to give students a sound introduction to where the sources of English law can be found and how laws are made, as well as differentiating between the different types of sources of law. The unit examines the law-making role of judges through the doctrine of precedent and the process of statutory interpretation, the role of Parliament through Acts and through delegated legislation, and the increasing influence of European Union law on English law.

There are three sections in this guide:
- **Introduction** — this section gives advice on how to use the guide, some learning strategies, some hints on planning revision, a reminder of the assessment criteria and how to achieve them, and also an explanation of what the exam paper is about and the skills needed to complete it successfully.
- **Content Guidance** — this sets out the specification content for Unit G152 and the key knowledge for successful completion of the exam. It is broken down into sections in the same way as the specification and provides a structure for your learning. Where cases or statutes are referred to, you will need to study these in more detail for a fuller understanding. This is the one unit in the AS course where detailed knowledge of cases is essential.
- **Questions and Answers** — this section provides sample answers to typical examination questions on each topic area. Each question is followed by an A-, a C- and an E-grade answer. Examiner comments show how marks are awarded or why they are withheld.

How to use this guide

The Content Guidance section covers all the elements of the Unit G152 specification, breaking down each topic into manageable sections for initial study and later revision. It is not intended to be a comprehensive and detailed set of notes for the unit — the material needs to be supplemented by further reading from textbooks and by your own class notes.

At the end of each topic section, you may find it useful to compile a summary of the factual material under appropriate headings. Ideally, you should incorporate additional material drawn from a number of sources: classroom teaching, textbooks, quality newspapers, law journals and legal websites. When you have finished compiling your notes, you can tackle the questions in the third section of the guide. Read the questions carefully and answer them fully. You should then read the sample A-grade answers and compare these with your own answers to identify where you could have picked up more marks to gain a higher grade. Your answers can also be compared with the

C-grade or E-grade answers in order to get an indication of how well you are performing. The examiner comments will help you to achieve an understanding of what can limit your marks and how to attain the higher grades. The additional examiner comments which appear at the end of each set of answers will help you to appreciate what is included in the source that you could make use of in your answer, and the sort of information that you ought to include which is not contained in the source.

Learning strategies

To be successful at AS you need good knowledge and understanding of the various topics that you have studied during your course. Keep a clear and accurate set of notes. To help you:

- Try to take notes in class in a logical and methodical way and don't just write down everything that the teacher says.
- Make sure that you go back and read your notes again after each class and don't leave it too long or the information will not be fresh in your mind.
- If you don't understand something in your notes, read about it in your textbook or ask for advice from your teacher and then make sure that you alter your notes so that they are correct and you can understand them.
- Complete all the reading that your teacher suggests and also try to read around the subject to build up greater knowledge and understanding. If you have spaces in your class notes, you can add additional information from your reading. If not, you should rewrite your notes to incorporate it.
- Use a legal dictionary so that you are familiar with all the appropriate legal terminology.

Revision planning

Revision is not the same thing as learning. All of the learning strategies mentioned above should have been covered during the course and you should have a complete and accurate set of notes when you begin your revision. If you have to learn the material from scratch, then you are putting extra pressure on yourself.

There are various rules for good revision practice which you should follow:

- Organise your material before you begin your revision. You will be revising more than one subject and you will have many topics to study in each subject. It will help your revision process if you have separate folders for each subject and use folder dividers for individual topics. That way you can turn straight to the topic you wish to revise.
- Organise your time effectively. A half hour or so preparing a revision timetable at the start will save you a lot of time later on. Divide the time you have available by the topic areas, identify how many times you can revise them and then create a chart.
- Use revision aids to help compress the subject matter or put it into visual form to make the process simpler and less time consuming. Examples are key facts charts, mind maps, flowcharts and diagrams.

- Use your friends or family to test you on important knowledge.
- Practise past papers. The more familiar you are with the style of questions that come up, the more confidence you will have in answering them in the exam.
- Do your revision in short bursts. The longer you sit looking at your notes in one session, the more likely you are to get bored and not take anything in. Take plenty of breaks between sessions.

Assessment objectives

Assessment objectives (AOs) are the measures against which examiners test your knowledge, understanding and legal skills. They are common to AS and A2 units and are intended to assess a candidate's ability to:

- AO1 — recall, select and develop knowledge and understanding of legal principles accurately and by means of example and citation, i.e. your ability to remember the appropriate law, including cases or statutes where appropriate.
- AO2 — analyse legal material, issues and situations, and evaluate and apply the appropriate legal rules and principles, i.e. your ability to engage in a balanced discussion and to offer points of criticism in essays, and to apply legal rules to factual situations in problem-style questions.
- AO3 — present a logical and coherent argument and communicate relevant material in a clear and effective manner, using appropriate legal terminology, i.e. your ability to give legal information and to discuss or apply it clearly, as well as to spell, punctuate and use grammar accurately.

The examination

Unit G152 offers a choice of two questions, both based on source materials. Each question is split into three parts and students are required to answer all parts.

- Part (a) is a pure knowledge-based question deriving from information in the source material and is worth 15 marks which are from AO1 (12 marks) and AO3 (3 marks).
- Part (b) is a pure application question of material in the source, again worth 15 marks, and for which only AO2 marks are available.
- Part (c) is a discussion question worth 30 marks, with 15 AO1 marks in part (i), and 12 AO2 marks and 3 AO3 marks in part (ii). This question is always split into two parts. It is the one out of all AS papers that most resembles what you are asked to do in essay questions at A2. Again, the question is derived from information that is to be found in the source material.

Planning is an important part of achieving high marks in any examination. With the Sources of Law paper it is even more so. The source materials are provided to help you and you can get better marks by using the information in them. Before you begin to answer any of the parts of a question, you should highlight or underline key points in the sources that you can use in your answers. Then you will not have to read the whole source again when you need the information. You could also identify for which part of the questions each highlighted section will be useful by writing (a), (b) or (c) in the margin next to it.

You can make brief plans as you would for Unit G151, so that you include information that you know but which is not in the sources. This will help you to achieve higher marks. Remember, part (b) questions are all about applying information given in the sources to factual situations, so it is impossible to give an appropriate answer without specifically using the sources. Be selective in what you write. If a question on precedent is all about the Practice Statement, then you have no need to write about the rules in *Young* v *Bristol Aeroplane* on the Court of Appeal. Unlike Unit G151, in this unit different amounts of time need to be allocated to different parts of the question. Parts (a) and (b) are each worth half the marks of part (c). You should therefore spend a quarter of your time on each of parts (a) and (b) and half of your time on part (c).

Content
Guidance

The material covered in Unit G152 is divided into five sections. They are all concerned with how the law is formed and where it can be found. The fifth section, 'Law reform', is less important than the others since at most it only forms part of a question. The other sections should be studied in detail. The sections covered are:

Doctrine of precedent: mechanics and law-making potential
- The nature and importance of precedent
- The elements of a case
- The hierarchy of the courts
- Binding and persuasive precedent
- Ways of avoiding precedent
- The House of Lords and the Practice Statement 1966
- The Court of Appeal
- The advantages and disadvantages of precedent

Legislation
- Stages leading to legislation
- The different types of bill
- The stages in the passing of an Act of Parliament
- Delegated legislation
- The types of delegated legislation
- The controls on delegated legislation
- The advantages and disadvantages of delegated legislation

Statutory interpretation
- The two approaches
- The three rules
- The language rules
- Presumptions
- Intrinsic and extrinsic aids

European Union law
- Law-making functions of the Council, the Commission and Parliament
- The composition and role of the European Court of Justice
- Primary, secondary and tertiary sources of European Union law
- The impact of European Union law on national law, supremacy and direct effect

Law reform
- Purpose of law reform
- Impetus for law reform
- Law reform agencies

Doctrine of precedent: mechanics and law-making potential

The nature and importance of precedent

Precedent is a feature of all common-law jurisdictions. The doctrine of precedent is based on the Latin maxim *stare decisis* (or more precisely *stare rationibus decidendis*), meaning to stand by what has been decided and not unsettling what is already established law. This means that where the material facts of a present case are similar to those in a previously decided case, the judge is bound to apply the principle of law used in the decided case to the present case. The doctrine of precedent rests on two key principles:

- All cases involving similar facts to decided cases should be judged on the basis of the existing principles from those decided cases.
- Courts are bound by the precedents from cases decided in courts that are higher than them or of equal status to them.

In the English legal system, the doctrine is adhered to more rigidly than in other jurisdictions. This can be illustrated by two cases decided by the same judges in the same court on the same day. In *Re Schweppes Ltd's Agreement* (1965) Lord Justice Willmer dissented and thus disagreed with the principle being applied by the other judges. In *Re Automatic Telephone and Electric Co Ltd's Agreement* (1965) he gave the leading judgement, and even though he had dissented in the earlier case, he felt himself bound by the principle and applied it.

Sometimes an appeal court creates an original precedent. This is where there is no existing law on the issue (e.g. *Airedale NHS Trust* v *Bland*, 1993).

The elements of a case

Precedents that must be followed in later cases come from principles of law that are found in existing cases. There are two key elements in the judgements of cases:

- The **ratio decidendi**. This means the reason for the decision. Professor Zander defines it as the principle of law that decided the case in the light of the material facts. A *ratio* may simply extend or develop the previous law but it can also be 'original', which means that there was no previous law on the particular issue. The *ratio* is the binding part of the judgement where the law is found and that provides precedent for judges to follow in later cases. It is, of course, possible to find more than one *ratio* in a case. It is also sometimes not easy to find the *ratio*. An example of this is *R* v *Dudley & Stephens* (1884).

- Judges also make other statements in their judgements that are not the principle of law deciding the case. These are known as **obiter dicta**, which means 'things said by the way'. Judges may, for instance, say what the law might be if the facts of the case were slightly different. An example of this is the acceptance in the case of *Hedley Byrne* v *Heller & Partners* (1964) that there could be liability for a negligent misstatement causing a purely financial loss. Statements made *obiter* can still be influential on later judges, particularly if they are made by high-ranking judges, such as those in the House of Lords.

The hierarchy of the courts

There is a strict hierarchy of courts in the English legal system. Courts are bound to follow the precedents of those courts equal to or above them within this hierarchy. It is generally only the higher appeal courts that are capable of creating precedents which other courts are then bound to follow.

The European Court of Justice

European Union (EU) law does not affect every area of English law. Where it does, however, since 1 January 1973 the European Court of Justice (ECJ) is the highest court and decisions of the court are binding on all courts in England and Wales, although not on itself. An example is *Macarthy's Ltd* v *Smith* (1980), where the ECJ disagreed with the House of Lords on the issue of a woman claiming equal pay with a man who previously did her job.

The House of Lords

- The House of Lords is the highest court in England and Wales.
- It is bound to follow decisions of the ECJ.
- All courts below are bound by its decisions.
- Traditionally the House of Lords was bound by its own past decisions following *London Street Tramways* v *London County Council* (1898), which approved the rule set in *Beamish* v *Beamish* (1861). It could only overrule its previous decisions if they were decided *per incuriam* (without applying appropriate case law or statute) or if they were inconsistent with statute law.
- Since the introduction of the Practice Statement 1966, the House of Lords can overrule its past decisions when 'it appears right to do so'.

The Court of Appeal

- The Court of Appeal is made up of two divisions: the Civil Division and the Criminal Division.
- Each division is bound to follow the decisions of the ECJ and the House of Lords.
- Each division also binds the respective civil and criminal courts below it.

- The Court is generally bound by its own past decisions except in certain circum-stances identified in *Young* v *Bristol Aeroplane* (1944) and with more flexibility in the Criminal Division.

The divisional courts

- The term 'divisional court' is used to refer to one of the three divisions of the High Court (Family, Chancery and Queen's Bench) acting as an appeal court or in a supervisory capacity.
- The divisional courts are bound by the ECJ, the House of Lords and the Court of Appeal.
- They also bind all lower courts.
- They are generally bound by their own past decisions but with some flexibility similar to that exercised by the Court of Appeal.

The High Court

- The High Court is also a civil trial court, again separated into three divisions.
- It is bound by all the courts above, including the divisional courts.
- Each division is not generally bound by itself or by the decisions of other High Court judges but it is common for these to be followed.

The inferior courts

The other courts — the Crown Court, the County Court, and the Magistrates' Court — are bound by the decisions of the higher courts. However, they do not themselves create any precedent. Decisions of a High Court judge sitting in the Crown Court can be persuasive.

Binding and persuasive precedent

There are generally said to be two types of precedent: binding precedent and persuasive precedent.

Binding precedent

A binding precedent is a principle of law that must be followed by the court in a later case if the material facts in the case are similar, even if the judges do not agree with the principle in the case.

Binding precedent can only come from the *ratio decidendi* of the past case. The *ratio* is only binding on the present case if the facts of this case are sufficiently similar to those in the case in which the precedent is found, and if the precedent were made in a court equal or higher in the hierarchy of courts.

Persuasive precedent

Persuasive precedent is not binding on a future court, i.e. it does not have to be followed. However, it may influence a judge in a later case who may wish to apply the principle. This may happen, for instance, when in the present case there is no obvious binding precedent to follow.

Persuasive precedent comes from a variety of sources. These include:

- **Obiter dicta from a decided case.** For example, the *obiter* comments in *Rondel* v *Worsley* (1969) *1 AC 191* were later applied by the court in *Saif Ali* v *Sidney Mitchell & Co* (1978) *3 WLR 849*.
- **Dissenting judgements** (statements made in an appeal case by a judge who disagrees with the principles stated by the majority judges and who wishes to state what he thinks the law should be). These are sometimes followed in later cases if they have been made by sufficiently senior judges. For example, the House of Lords eventually followed Lord Denning's dissenting judgement from *Candler* v *Crane Christmas & Co* (1951) in *Hedley Byrne* v *Heller & Partners* (1964).
- **Minority judgements** (these are additional comments in a case made by the judges who do not give the leading judgement).
- **Judgements made in the Privy Council and in other Commonwealth courts**, e.g. the definition of remoteness of damage for negligence from *The Wagon Mound (No 1)* (1961) that damage must be foreseeable is now the standard test.
- **The works of leading academics.** For example, the House of Lords in *Dunlop* v *Selfridge* (1915) approved Sir Frederick Pollock's definition of consideration contained in his book *Principles of Contract* that 'an act of forbearance or the promise thereof is the price for which the promise of the other is bought, and the promise thus given for value is enforceable'.

In fact courts do not always rigidly follow the rules regarding their position in the hierarchy. For instance in *R* v *Holley* (2005), the Privy Council, hearing an appeal from Jersey, decided that the House of Lords was wrong in *R* v *Smith (Morgan James)* (2000) on the issue of loss of self-control in the defence of provocation in murder. In fact the Privy Council should have followed *Smith*. In *R* v *James, R* v *Karimi* (2006), the Court of Appeal (Criminal Division) chose to apply *Holley* rather than *Smith* and held that, in very exceptional circumstances, a decision of the Privy Council can take precedence over a decision of the House of Lords. It justified this on the grounds that the Privy Council in *Holley* was made up of 9 of the 12 judges from the House of Lords and, as it was decided six to three, the majority of the House of Lords wished the rule in *Smith* to be changed. The Court of Appeal in effect overruled the precedent of a higher court by applying a precedent that could only be persuasive.

Ways of avoiding precedent

There are a limited number of ways that enable courts to avoid binding precedent:

- **Overruling** — where an appeal court decides in a later case that the precedent from the older case was wrong.

- **Reversing** — where in a case being appealed a higher court changes the decision from the court below.
- **Distinguishing** — this process, available to all courts, is where a court decides that the material facts of the present case are sufficiently different from the precedent that the court is being asked to apply, e.g. the principle in *Balfour* v *Balfour* (1919) on the presumption against legal intention in contract law in the case of social and domestic agreements was not applied in *Merritt* v *Merritt* (1971).

The House of Lords and the Practice Statement 1966

Under the Practice Statement 1966, the House of Lords has the power to depart from its previous decisions 'when it appears right to do so'. This is to avoid injustice and to allow the law to develop. Nevertheless, judges in the House of Lords must bear in mind the danger of disturbing retrospectively the basis on which contracts, settlements, property arrangements and tax arrangements have been made, and must also recognise the special need for certainty in criminal law. The Practice Statement only gives this power to the House of Lords.

However, the House of Lords has rarely used its powers. It has even shown reluctance where the judges think that the law may lead to injustice, e.g. in *Jones* v *Secretary of State for Social Services* (1972) it would not overrule the decision in *Re Dowling* (1967), even though the judges all felt that this would lead to injustice and most felt the case had been wrongly decided.

The Practice Statement 1966 was first used in *Conway* v *Rimmer* (1968) to overrule *Duncan* v *Cammell Laird Shipbuilders* (1942), but only on a technical point. The first major use to avoid injustice was in *BR Board* v *Herrington* (1972), overruling *Addie* v *Dumbreck* (1929) on the duty of care owed to a child trespasser.

It has been used to correct what judges see as errors in the law, as in *Murphy* v *Brentwood DC* (1990) overruling the two-part test for negligence from *Anns* v *Merton LBC* (1977).

It has also been used to react to modern circumstances, as in *Milliangos* v *George Frank Textiles* (1976) which, in overruling *Re Havana Railways* (1961), permitted damages to be awarded in a currency other than sterling. Similarly, *R* v *R (Marital Rape)* (1991) changed the outdated rule that a man could not be prosecuted for raping his wife. It has also been used to improve the practice of statutory interpretation in *Pepper* v *Hart* (1993), overruling *Davis* v *Johnson* (1978) on the use of *Hansard*.

The Practice Statement 1966 was not used in criminal law for 20 years until *R* v *Shivpuri* (1986) overruled *Anderton* v *Ryan* (1985) on impossible attempts, and this was only to correct an error of the House of Lords. It was used to limit the defence of duress in *R* v *Howe* (1987), overruling *DPP for Northern Ireland* v *Lynch* (1975). More recently the case of *R* v *G & R* (2003) has done away with the much-criticised objective recklessness from *R* v *Caldwell* (1982).

The Court of Appeal

The Court of Appeal is usually bound by its own past precedent, subject to the exceptions in *Young* v *Bristol Aeroplane Co. Ltd* (1944):
- Where there are two conflicting past Court of Appeal decisions it may choose one and reject the other.
- Where a Court of Appeal decision, though not overruled, is inconsistent with a later decision of the House of Lords, then it must follow the House of Lords' decision.
- Where a Court of Appeal decision was made *per incuriam* (or without reference to all the appropriate authorities), then it may ignore that decision.

More recently, the Court can go against a precedent which conflicts with the **Human Rights Act 1998**. The Criminal Division of the Court of Appeal can also avoid its own decisions if the law has been 'misapplied or misunderstood' because of the possible loss of liberty, as in *R* v *Taylor* (1950) and *R* v *Gould* (1968).

The advantages and disadvantages of precedent

Precedent is an essential feature of the English legal system. Its advantages and disadvantages seem to focus on the contrast between certainty and flexibility.

Advantages
- Certainty is gained when legal principles are followed absolutely.
- This retains uniformity and predictability in the law.
- It prevents unnecessary litigation.
- Lawyers can advise their clients with confidence.
- Settlements are more likely.
- The cost of litigation is consequently reduced.
- There is said to be sufficient flexibility for the law to develop because of the different ways of avoiding precedent, particularly the Practice Statement.
- The law is allowed to grow naturally.
- There is a wealth of detailed principles contained in the law reports.
- The doctrine respects the right of Parliament as the supreme law maker.

Disadvantages
- The law may be prevented from growing and developing because of the rigidity of the system.

- There is some uncertainty because it is not always easy to find the *ratio* of a case.
- The House of Lords rarely uses the Practice Statement to change the law and other courts are denied the same flexibility.
- Injustice can be caused or the law can become outdated, as in *R* v *R* (1991) where the principle had been maintained for 200 years.
- The lack of flexibility leads to judges distinguishing on spurious grounds.
- Inconvenience and extra cost can be caused because there are so many decided cases and the appropriate law may be hard to find.

Legislation

Stages leading to legislation

Stimulus for legislation comes from various places. It can result from the manifesto of the governing party when elected. Pressure for change can come from MPs in the governing party on issues of national concern. It can also come from a variety of pressure groups and from public pressure generally.

The government may then seek the opinions of interested parties by issuing a Green Paper, a general consultation document. Interested parties can respond to this and any amendments that are acceptable can be made. All evidence is then collated, amendments are added, and government policy is expressed in a White Paper.

Once specific legislative proposals have been agreed, these are then drafted by parliamentary counsel (government lawyers) in the form of a bill for presentation to Parliament. The bill is put before Parliament, usually before the House of Commons first. Some non-controversial bills are put before the House of Lords first.

The different types of bill

All Acts of Parliament begin life as bills. There are three different types of bill that may be put before Parliament:
- public bills
- private bills
- private members' bills

Public bills

These are bills that seek to alter the general law. They are the most common type of bill and are usually introduced by the government as a means of implementing government policy.

Private bills

These are bills that are introduced on behalf of or affect only one part of the community or a specific organisation seeking special powers. Such bills were used in the nineteenth century to permit the building of the railways. The same type of bill was then used when the railways were taken into public ownership in the twentieth century. Before the introduction of more general laws, this was the same type of bill that would be used to dissolve a marriage.

Private members' bills

Members of Parliament, whether in the House of Commons or the House of Lords, are entitled to introduce their own bills into Parliament. Time for debate is much more restricted than for other bills, so only 20 are selected by a vote out of all those that are put forward. Usually they fail because they run out of debating time before a vote can be taken on them. For instance, there were 14 separate private members' bills on disability discrimination before the **Disability Discrimination Act 1995** was passed. However, on occasions such bills concern issues of great importance and sometimes become law when they are adopted by the government of the day. This was the case with the **Abortion Act 1967**, which resulted from David Steel's private members' bill.

The stages in the passing of an Act of Parliament

Before a bill becomes law as an Act of Parliament it has to pass through a number of different stages and be voted on. This is why the law-making process is seen as democratic.

A bill has to go before both Houses of Parliament but can start in either the House of Commons or the House of Lords. In practice, most bills commence in the House of Commons, where they go through five stages.

House of Commons (or House of Lords)

First reading
This is when the bill is formally presented to Parliament. The title of the bill is read out to the House and it is then printed and published.

Second reading
The MP introducing the bill, usually a government minister, explains the purposes of the bill and proposes it. There follows a full debate in which all members are allowed to take part. When the debate has finished, a vote is taken. If the vote is against the bill, it will proceed no further at this stage. If the vote is for the bill to continue, it passes on to the committee stage.

Committee stage

A standing committee of MPs is selected from all parties but chosen on the basis of party strength. The committee discusses the bill in detail and examines every clause closely. Amendments are sometimes introduced and voted on by the committee. When the committee is satisfied with the bill in its new form, it is returned to the House.

Report stage

Representatives of the committee then report the bill in its new form, including any amendments, to the House. Other MPs can suggest additional amendments and all of these are debated and voted on.

Third reading

The bill is now introduced in its final form with all amendments made in the earlier stages. A final vote is taken and if the bill is passed, it is then scrutinised in the House of Lords.

House of Lords (or House of Commons)

If the bill is passed on to the other House, it goes through the same five stages in that House as it did in the other. If a bill is amended in the House of Lords, then it will be passed back to the House of Commons for consideration of these amendments.

Because of the Parliament Acts, the House of Lords only has the power to delay the passage of legislation, not to reject it completely.

Once the House of Lords has voted on and accepted the bill, it is passed on for the final part of the process before it becomes law.

The royal assent

Every bill that has come successfully through the different stages in both Houses has to receive approval from the Queen before it can become law. This is known as the royal assent. In practice it is a formality and the last time a monarch refused was in 1707. The speaker in each House announces that the bill has received royal assent and the bill then becomes an Act of Parliament and law.

Delegated legislation

Not all law can be made by Parliament through the democratic process. There simply is not the time available to debate and vote on all the laws that are made. Besides this, within the framework of basic policies many laws are technical and detailed. For this reason, Parliament delegates responsibility for introducing laws in particular areas. The law that results is known as delegated legislation.

The process allows for swifter response to necessary change. It also removes the need for extensive detail in Acts, it allows for specialists to draft the law made by this process and it saves debating time in Parliament.

Parliament often produces outline legislation and then leaves individual departments to add the more detailed rules. In this way, while around 100 Acts are passed each year, between 2,000 and 3,000 sets of regulations are introduced through delegated legislation.

The types of delegated legislation

There are three types of delegated legislation:
- statutory instruments
- Orders in Council
- bylaws

Statutory instruments

These are laws that are still passed in Parliament. They are also by far the most common form of delegated legislation.

Authority is given in an 'enabling' or 'parent' Act for a particular department or ministry to introduce specific and detailed regulations within the framework of the statute. They are common in areas of health and social welfare, employment, health and safety, and road traffic and transport. This is also the common way of introducing EU directives into English law. The lawyers in the appropriate department draft them and they are usually introduced by the ministers concerned.

Statutory instruments are not passed according to the usual parliamentary process but there are two possible procedures:
- **Affirmative resolution** — here there is a debate and vote on the regulation, but this procedure is rarely followed.
- **Negative resolution** — this is the most common procedure. The draft paper is left in one of the lobbies in Parliament for interested MPs to inspect and scrutinise. If no objections to the regulation are raised within a fixed period (usually 40 days), it automatically becomes law.

Orders in Council

Orders in Council are created by the Privy Council. They are generally used when the use of statutory instruments would be inappropriate or impossible in the circumstances. On this basis, their use is common in times of war or other emergencies. They are also used when there is a transfer of responsibility between different areas of government. The transfer of powers from Parliament to the assemblies in Scotland and Wales following devolution is an example of this.

The **Emergency Powers Act 1920** is an example of Parliament giving the Queen and the Privy Council the power to issue Orders in Council when Parliament is not sitting. The imposition of sanctions against Rhodesia (now Zimbabwe) in 1965 is an example of such an order being made in an emergency situation.

Bylaws

These are usually introduced by local councils and district councils, although they can also be introduced by statutory bodies requiring specific rules, for example those used to impose certain restrictions on public transport.

The fact that Parliament delegates power to local authorities allows these bodies to introduce legislation of limited scope on issues of purely local interest. Examples of this are parking restrictions, the playing of games on particular areas of grass, drinking in public places, and fouling of footpaths by dogs.

The controls on delegated legislation

Because laws made in this way are not subject to the democratic process, they obviously require greater scrutiny. As a result, unlike Acts of Parliament which can make and unmake any law and cannot be challenged by the courts, delegated legislation is subject to certain controls to ensure that the body making the law does not exceed or abuse its powers in any way.

There are two types of control of delegated legislation:
• control by Parliament
• control by the courts

Control by Parliament

All statutory instruments are limited by the power actually delegated in the enabling Act. Some Acts require that regulations are introduced by the affirmative resolution procedure, which is another control, but since most are introduced by the negative resolution procedure this is a fairly limited control.

The Delegated Powers Scrutiny Committee in the House of Lords reports back to the House before the committee stage on all delegated legislation which it sees as an inappropriate use of the delegated power. However, the committee has no power to make amendments and can only report its findings.

The most effective parliamentary control is the Scrutiny Committee (the Joint Select Committee on Statutory Instruments). This is an all-party committee which reviews all statutory instruments and can refer its findings back to either the House of Commons or the House of Lords for further consideration. It will usually do this when the delegated legislation:
• introduces a tax (because only Parliament can do this)
• appears to have retrospective effect (unless this is indicated in the enabling Act)
• appears to have gone beyond the power granted in the enabling Act or uses the power granted in an unusual way
• is defective in some other way

Again, the committee has no power to amend the delegated legislation.

Under the **Legislative and Regulatory Reform Act 2006** there is now a super-affirmative resolution procedure. This enables more parties to be consulted and gives Parliament more control over delegated legislation.

Control by the courts

Control by the courts is through the process of judicial review in the Queen's Bench Division of the High Court. The court exercises this supervisory function over all administrative bodies, and all those acting in a judicial or quasi-judicial fashion. The court examines accusations of actions which are *ultra vires* (beyond the power of the body concerned) and those that offend the rules of natural justice (because there should be no decisions that are based on bias, and everyone has the right to a fair hearing).

There are two different types of *ultra vires*:
- **Substantive *ultra vires*** — this is where the body introducing the delegated legislation makes law that is beyond its powers to make. An example is *R* v *Secretary of State for Education and Employment, ex parte NUT* (2000) where conditions for teachers were set that were not within the powers given in the **Education Act 1996**.
- **Procedural *ultra vires*** — this is where the body has the power to introduce the law but has not followed the set procedures. An example is the *Aylesbury Mushroom* case (1972) where the minister failed to consult interested parties.

The court is also concerned with the concept of reasonableness following the case of *Associated Provincial Picture Houses* v *Wednesbury Corporation* (1948) where the court identified that decisions could not be valid where no reasonable person would have made them.

The advantages and disadvantages of delegated legislation

Advantages

- It saves parliamentary time.
- It allows for specialist expertise to be used in drafting the law.
- Technical detail can be avoided in enabling Acts.
- Regulations can be altered and updated without need for fresh enactment.
- It can be passed much more quickly than Acts of Parliament.
- It allows quick responses in emergency situations.
- It allows local knowledge to be used in drafting rules.
- It allows certain rules to fit local need.
- It can be easily revoked.

Disadvantages

- It is undemocratic.
- It lacks effective scrutiny.
- The process can be abused.
- It is not widely publicised.
- It is often sub-delegated to departments rather than being made by the minister.
- There is too much to keep up with and people may be unaware of it.

Statutory interpretation

Statutory interpretation is the process where judges are called on to give meaning to words in an Act of Parliament that are in dispute. Often there is no need for interpretation where the meaning of the words and the intention of Parliament when passing the Act are absolutely clear. However, there are several situations where interpretation may be necessary. These include:

- **Bad drafting** — the person drafting the Act uses the wrong word. In *Fisher* v *Bell* (1960) the words 'offer for sale' were used where 'invitation to treat' would have been the appropriate phrase in contract law. As a result, Parliament had to pass another Act.
- **Ambiguous words** — where the words have more than one meaning. In *R* v *Allen* (1872), applying the meaning 'being validly married' to the words 'shall marry' would have made the offence of bigamy unworkable. The court applied the words 'going through a marriage ceremony' instead.
- **Technical or legal meaning.** In *Beswick* v *Beswick* (1968) the words 'other property' were held to refer only to land and interests in land because that is what the Act in question concerned.
- **Social or technological developments** — because many things change over time or could not be contemplated when the legislation was passed. In *Royal College of Nursing* v *DHSS* (1981) the words 'registered medical practitioner' under the **Abortion Act 1967** required interpretation. The words could only mean a doctor. However, by the time of the case it was nurses rather than doctors who were carrying out the procedures and the House of Lords accepted that this was legal.
- **Broad terms** — an example of this is *Brock* v *DPP* (1993) where the words 'type of dog' were used and the problem was whether this referred only to breed or had a wider meaning.

Judges use various rules and aids in interpreting statutes and in all cases they are trying to find the intention of Parliament when the Act was passed. The problem is that the rules can produce very different results and therefore the process is unpredictable. Judges have at their disposal:

- two approaches
- three rules
- three language rules
- various presumptions
- intrinsic aids and extrinsic aids

The two approaches

- The **literal approach** is where interpretation relies mainly on the words in question without necessarily referring to anything else.
- The **purposive approach** is a modern approach resulting from membership of the EU and the style of interpretation that is favoured in Europe. The approach is concerned with discovering and giving effect to the purpose for which the legislation was passed and is not so preoccupied with the words in question. An example is *Royal College of Nursing* v *DHSS* (1981) where, even though the words 'registered medical practitioner' could only mean doctor, the House of Lords accepted that nurses could conduct a major role in abortions because the clear purpose of the **Abortion Act 1967** was to ensure that abortions were carried out under clinical conditions.

The three rules

The literal rule

This rule, preferred for most of the nineteenth and twentieth centuries, demands that the words should be given their 'plain, ordinary literal meaning...even though this might lead to a manifest absurdity' as stated by Lord Esher in *R* v *City of London Court* (1892).

The problem is that words do not always have plain meanings or they may have ambiguous meanings so that absurdities can occur, as in *Whiteley* v *Chappell* (1868) where an election fraud went unpunished because it was held that a dead man would not be 'entitled to vote'.

Focusing only on the words themselves can also lead to illogical results as in *IRC* v *Hinchey* (1960) where the judges ignored tax that had already been paid in their interpretation of the words 'three times the amount owed'. It can also mean that Parliament has to pass another Act to get over the difficulty, as in *Fisher* v *Bell* (1960).

More importantly it can lead to injustices occurring. A classic example is *London & North Eastern Railway* v *Berriman* (1946) where a widow was denied compensation for the death of her husband. He was killed while oiling points on a railway line, and compensation was only payable if he had been 'relaying or repairing' the line. The court held that 'relaying or repairing' did not include 'maintenance', taking the words of the Fatal Accidents Act literally.

In *Magor & St Mellons* v *Newport Corporation* (1950), Lord Denning was critical of the literal rule and suggested that instead judges should use the mischief rule and 'fill in the gaps' if necessary. He was criticised in the House of Lords where Lord Simonds called this a 'naked usurpation of the legislative function'.

The Law Commission has also been critical of the literal rule. In its 1969 report it argued that 'to place undue emphasis on the literal meaning of words is to assume an unattainable perfection in draftsmanship'.

The golden rule

The golden rule is, in fact, a subsidiary of the literal rule, so it is only used by judges who prefer to use the literal rule. It is also only used where using the literal rule would lead to an absurdity. Lord Blackburn explained the golden rule in *River Weir Commissioners* v *Adamson* (1877) as 'giving the words their ordinary signification, unless when so applied they produce an absurdity or inconvenience so great as to convince the court that the intention could not have been to use them in their ordinary signification and to justify the court in putting on them some other signification'.

The rule can be used in one of two ways:
- **The narrow approach** — here, if the word in question is ambiguous and using the plain meaning can lead to absurdity, the judge will use another meaning which does not. An example is *R* v *Allen* (1872) where the plain meaning of the words would have prevented any convictions for the offence of bigamy and made the Act unworkable. Another example is *Adler* v *George* (1964) where the words 'in the vicinity of a prohibited place' were held to include 'in' the prohibited place, or again an illogical acquittal would have occurred.
- **The broad approach** — here the word is not ambiguous but giving it the plain meaning would prove unacceptable, so for policy reasons the judges prefer to give it a different meaning. The obvious example is *Re Sigsworth* (1935) where the court held that the word 'issue' did not include a person who had killed his parent so that the court was able to prevent a son inheriting from the mother that he had murdered.

The problem is that there are no real guidelines for when the rule should be used, which is why Professor Zander calls it an 'unpredictable safety valve'.

The mischief rule

This is the oldest of all the rules and it comes from *Heydon's Case* (1584) which outlined a four-point procedure:
- Examine the common law prior to the passing of the Act.
- Identify the 'mischief' or defect in the previous law.
- Identify the way in which Parliament proposed to remedy the defect.
- Give effect to it.

Examples include *Smith* v *Hughes* (1960) where 'public place or street' was held to include a first-floor balcony from which a prostitute was soliciting, in order to secure her conviction. *Corkery* v *Carpenter* (1951) is another example where, in recognition of technical changes since the Act was passed, 'carriage' was held to include 'bicycle' in order to protect other road users from drunks.

The language rules

There are also three language rules concerned with how words are applied in certain circumstances:

- **Noscitur a sociis** — meaning a word is known by the company it keeps. In *Beswick* v *Beswick* (1968) the words 'other property' were held to refer only to land or interests in land (referred to as real property by lawyers) because the words came from the **Law of Property Act 1925** which was only concerned with land.
- **Expressio unius est exclusio alterius** — meaning that the express mention of one thing in a list impliedly excludes other things not included in the list. In *Tempest* v *Kilner* (1846) a list in a section of an Act included 'goods, wares and merchandise'. As a result the section was held not to apply to 'stocks and shares' which had not been included in the list and thus could not have been intended to fall under the Act.
- **Ejusdem generis** — meaning 'of the same type'. The rule applies where there is a list of specific words that are then followed by general words. To fall within the scope of the provision, the general words have to be of the same type as the specific words. In *Powell* v *Kempton Park Racecourse* (1899), the words used were 'house, office, room or other place used for betting', so the provision could not apply to the outdoor betting area in question, as all the specific places in the list were indoor.

Presumptions

Judges often presume certain things to be true unless the contrary can be proved. Examples include:

- Parliament does not intend to change the common law unless it actually says so in the Act.
- In Acts creating criminal offences, *mens rea* (criminal intent) must always be proved unless the Act identifies the offence as one of strict liability not requiring intent (*Sweet* v *Parsley* (1970)).
- The Crown is not liable unless this is allowed for in the statute.
- The jurisdiction of the courts is not removed unless a specific alternative such as a tribunal is created and given jurisdiction by the Act.
- A person cannot be deprived of his/her liberty unless the Act specifically states this.
- A person will not be deprived of his/her property unless the Act states so.

- No retrospective laws are introduced unless Parliament specifically provides for this. The case of *Burmah Oil* v *The Lord Advocate* (1965) concerning the **War Damages Act 1965** is an example.

Intrinsic and extrinsic aids

Judges also have different aids that they can use to help them in interpreting words in statutes. These can be either:
- **intrinsic (internal) aids** that can be found inside the statute itself
- **extrinsic (external) aids** that are outside the statute

Intrinsic aids

These are found inside the Act and can be used by a judge using any of the rules, although some judges preferring the literal rule focus on the words even without using such aids. There are several intrinsic aids:
- **The short title** — this is merely the name of the Act, so while it gives a clue as to what the Act concerns it is probably of only minor assistance in interpretation.
- **The long title** — some statutes have a long title at the front of the Act which explains what the Act is trying to achieve in a sort of list of objectives, so it can prove quite useful in interpretation.
- **The preamble** — older Acts contained a detailed preamble at the front detailing what the statute covered and what it intended to achieve.
- **Margin notes** — these are included afterwards by the person drafting the Act and so are not strictly speaking part of it. They sometimes indicate the purpose of a section.
- **Schedules** — these usually come at the end of a section and often include more detailed information. An example is Schedule 2 of the **Unfair Contract Terms Act 1977** which details tests for determining reasonableness.
- **Headings** — some sections have headings which can be a guide when there is ambiguity.
- **Interpretation sections** — these are a major aid to interpretation, often giving the meaning of the technical words used. A good example is sections 2–6 of the **Theft Act 1968** which explain the terms used in the offence of theft in s.1 of the Act.

Extrinsic aids

These are found outside the Act and tend to be used more by judges favouring a purposive approach to interpretation. Some of them have proved controversial:
- **Dictionaries** — even judges using the literal rule are often prepared to use a dictionary to find the plain meaning of a word.
- **Other statutes** — these can be useful where Acts are drafted in similar terms. The **Sex Discrimination Act 1975** and the **Race Relations Act 1976**, for instance, are written in almost identical terms.

- **Royal Commission reports** — these can be useful where the commission has led to the legislation.
- **Law Commission reports** — the Law Commission often prepares draft bills and researches areas of law with a view to reform. If these precede the legislation, they can be a useful aid.
- *Hansard* — this is the official detailed report of the debates on the bill in the House of Commons and the House of Lords, so it is extremely useful in finding Parliament's intention when passing the Act. However, judges formerly condemned its use, as was seen by the rebukes received by Lord Denning in *Davis* v *Johnson* (1978). Now, following *Pepper* v *Hart* (1993) *Hansard* can be used if certain conditions are met.
- *Travaux preparatoires* — these are preparatory notes for treaties and can be used, for instance, when Acts based on EU law need to be interpreted.

European Union law

The European Union (EU) is currently made up of 27 different member states: Austria, Belgium, Bulgaria, Cyprus, the Czech Republic, Denmark, Estonia, Finland, France, Germany, Greece, Hungary, Ireland, Italy, Latvia, Lithuania, Luxembourg, Malta, the Netherlands, Poland, Portugal, Romania, Slovakia, Slovenia, Spain, Sweden and the UK.

The influence of the EU is mainly in economic areas. However, the EU is also a legal order and all member states are bound to follow the law that arises from EU treaties and their secondary legislation. For this reason the EU has both political and legal institutions that develop laws in furtherance of the objectives of the treaties.

There are four key institutions:
- the Council of Ministers (there is also a twice-yearly conference of heads of member states called the European Council, which is concerned with developing policy)
- the Commission
- the European Parliament
- the European Court of Justice (ECJ) — supported by the Court of First Instance (CFI)

Law-making functions of the Council, the Commission and Parliament

The Council of Ministers

This is the real law-making body of the EU. It has been said that 'the Commission proposes and the Council disposes'. This means that, although it is the Commission that prepares draft legislation in keeping with the aims of the treaties, it is the Council of Ministers that actually has the power to pass legislation.

Membership of the Council of Ministers is fluid. The composition of meetings depends on the topic to be discussed so, for example, a meeting on agricultural issues will be attended by the minister for agriculture from each member state.

Legislation is passed according to a very particular type of voting system. The voting system depends on whether the provision is to change or develop the treaties, as was the case with the so-called Maastricht Treaty (the Treaty on European Union) which created the EU. In such cases a unanimous vote is required. For the majority of legislation a qualified majority voting system is used. Votes are distributed among the member states according to their size and importance and the qualified majority is set at a figure that ensures smaller states have a say in the outcome.

The Commission

The Commission is like a civil service. Each member state appoints a commissioner but the Commission also includes all the specialist staff that make up the various departments. The individual departments have responsibility for introducing policy and preparing draft legislation in the form of regulations and directives.

The Commission has three key responsibilities:

- **Initiating legislation** — the Commission puts forward draft proposals for legislation on anything covered by the treaties, which it then presents to Parliament and the Council.
- **Enforcing EU law** — the Commission is often referred to as the 'watchdog' of the treaties. All member states are bound to follow and to achieve the objectives of the treaties. The Commission has the responsibility to ensure that all member states apply EU law properly. It can deal with breaches of EU law by member states by taking action in the ECJ.
- **Implementing the EU budget** — the Commission has executive functions and manages the EU budget, even though it is national and local authorities that usually spend the money. For example, the Commission has supervisory responsibility for the European Social Fund.

The Commission is also able to introduce some legislation, such as the issuing of decisions in the case of breaches of EU competition law.

The European Parliament

The European Parliament was originally called the Assembly, and at one time it had little influence on the introduction of law.

However, it is now an elected and representative body, and the only truly democratic institution in the EU. The number of MEPs (Members of the European Parliament) that each member state has depends on its size and importance.

Because of the Single European Act, the Treaty on European Union, the Treaty of Amsterdam and the Treaty of Nice, Parliament has been given a greater involvement in the legislative process.

It currently has three main powers:

- **It plays an important part in legislation** — under the co-decision procedure, now probably the most common method of introducing legislation, all draft legislation must go before Parliament. It can make amendments and in some cases can even prevent the draft legislation from becoming law.
- **It has a supervisory role over some EU institutions** — an example is its ability to pass a motion of censure on the Commission. This happened in 1999 when it caused the resignation of the entire Commission.
- **It has powers over the 'non-compulsory' budget** — Parliament has to approve the annual budget. This is an impressive power because the budget includes the day-to-day payment of all of the officials in the institutions.

The composition and role of the European Court of Justice

Composition of the ECJ

The European Court of Justice (ECJ) is staffed by Judges-Rapporteurs and Advocates-General who assist them by providing reasoned opinions. There is one judge for every member state and there are eight Advocates-General. The judges are selected from high-level judges from the member states but they must all be impartial and must all swear an oath as such.

Role of the ECJ

The role of the ECJ and the Court of First Instance (CFI) to ensure that the law is observed in the interpretation and application of the treaty is identified in Article 220 of the European Community (EC) Treaty.

The ECJ has three key objectives in its work:

- to ensure that in application and interpretation the law is observed
- to provide a forum in which to resolve disputes between the institutions, the member states, and also individuals
- to ensure that individual rights are protected

The ECJ is not like the courts in the English legal system and it hears five main types of action:

- Article 234 references from member states — these are for a preliminary ruling on an interpretation of EU law and will be binding on the case in the member state

- Article 226 actions against member states that are in breach of their treaty obligations
- Article 230 actions against EU institutions that abuse the power given them in the treaties
- Article 232 actions against EU institutions where they have failed to act as they should
- Article 288 actions for damages against EU institutions that have caused a loss to an individual either by a failure to act or by an abuse of power

The ECJ is now supported by the CFI. The CFI was created in order to reduce the workload of the ECJ and to prevent the backlog of cases that was building up. The CFI hears specific types of cases but its role has now expanded.

Primary, secondary and tertiary sources of European Union law

Primary

The primary source of EU law is the treaties themselves. The EC Treaty includes three main types of provisions:
- It defines the powers of the various EU institutions.
- It defines the rights and obligations of the member states.
- It sets out the treaty objectives.

Within the objectives, the treaty also provides a body of substantive law. Examples of this include free movement of workers under Article 39 and equal pay under Article 141. All member states are bound to give effect to the treaty Articles.

Secondary

The different types of legislation of the EU are defined and authorised in Article 249. There are three main types of legislation:
- regulations
- directives
- decisions

Regulations
These are general legislative measures building on the provisions in the treaties. They are identified as being generally applicable, meaning that they apply throughout the EU, and directly applicable, meaning that they automatically become law in member states without any need for further enactment. They are also binding in their entirety. An example is Regulation 1612/68 which builds on Article 39 and sets out the rights of workers' families.

Directives

These are legislative measures for the purpose of harmonising the law in member states. They are identified as being binding as to the result to be achieved. This means that they are, in effect, an order to member states to introduce national law that will achieve the objectives contained in the directive. They therefore require implementation by member states and this must be done within set time limits. An example is Directive 64/221 which identifies exemptions under Article 39 of public policy, public security and public health, on which member states can rely to avoid free movement.

Decisions

These are binding in their entirety on parties to whom they are addressed and they are usually addressed to specific individuals, for example where there has been a breach of EU competition law.

Tertiary

The case law of the ECJ is one source of law which must be followed. There are a number of general principles of law which the judges in the ECJ also apply in cases. These include:

- **Proportionality** — no burden should be placed on a citizen except to the extent that it is necessary to achieve the objective and is proportional.
- **Equality** — there should be no discrimination between people or groups of people.
- **Legal certainty** — there should be no violation of legitimate expectations.
- **Protection of human rights** — there should be uniform application of law.
- **Subsidiarity** — the institutions of the EU will not act where a better result can be achieved at national level in the member states.

The impact of European Union law on national law, supremacy and direct effect

Supranationalism

The EU depends on the concept of supranationalism. This, in effect, means that the law of the EU and the institutions of the EU are superior to national law, and national institutions are bound to follow EU law.

UK membership

UK membership of first the EC and later the EU came as a result of signing the original three treaties — the European Coal and Steel Community Treaty (ECSC), the European Atomic Energy Community Treaty (EURATOM) and the EC Treaty — but also as a result of the passing of the **European Communities Act 1972**. This membership began on 1 January 1973.

Probably the most important section of the Act is s. 2(1) which states that 'All such rights, powers, liabilities, obligations and restrictions from time to time created by or arising under the treaties, and all such remedies and procedures from time to time provided for by or under the treaties...are without further enactment to be given legal effect'. In other words, when the UK became a member it accepted that it would be bound by all current and all future EU law.

Membership has been affected by the passing of the subsequent treaties such as the **Single European Act 1986**, the Treaty on European Union 1992, the Treaty of Amsterdam 1997, and the Treaty of Nice 2000.

Supremacy

The supranational character of the EU could not have been ensured without the member states accepting the legal order and accepting the superior nature of EU law. One way in which this has been achieved is through the concept of supremacy. The treaties themselves do not specifically mention supremacy. It is actually a creation of the ECJ through the case law. Supremacy means that in matters involving EU law this cannot be challenged by individual member states.

The case of *Van Gend & Loos* v *Netherlands Inland Revenue Administration* (1963) was the earliest statement of supremacy. Here the ECJ identified that a bulb grower who had suffered financially because of the introduction of a customs duty on imported fertilisers by the Dutch state could fight the measure using EU law, since the duty was contrary to provisions in the treaty. The ECJ held that the treaty had created a new legal order by which all member states had agreed to be bound by signing the treaties and had given up the right to legislate in certain areas.

Costa v *ENEL* (1964) provided another early statement of supremacy. The ECJ identified that all directly effective provisions of EU law would prevail over provisions of national law. Furthermore, in *Simmenthal* (1977) the ECJ held that it was the 'duty of national courts to give full effect to Treaty provisions and not to apply conflicting national law'.

More recently the most dramatic example of supremacy was in the case of *Factortame* (1990), where the ECJ held that member states' courts could suspend the operation of national legislation in order to comply with EU law. The ECJ held that: 'Community law must be interpreted as meaning that a national court which, in a case before it concerning Community law, considers that the sole obstacle which precludes it from granting interim relief is a rule of national law must set aside that rule.'

This position conflicts quite sharply with the UK view originally expressed by Lord Denning in *Macarthy's* v *Smith* (1979) where he stated: '...if the time should come when our Parliament deliberately passes an Act with the intention of repudiating the treaty or any provision in it or intentionally of acting inconsistently with it and says so in express terms, then I should have thought that it would be the duty of our courts to follow the statute of our Parliament.'

Direct effect

Direct effect is the mechanism that ensures supremacy, since it is the means by which rights created by EU law are enforceable by citizens of member states throughout the Community. The principle was first accepted by the ECJ in *Van Gend & Loos* v *Netherlands* (1963). The case identified the criteria for direct effect which are that the measure must be clear, precise, unconditional and non-dependent.

Treaty articles and regulations are directly applicable throughout the EU, without need for further enactment. They may also be directly effective if they provide rights enforceable by a citizen in his own national court and conform to the *Van Gend & Loos* test.

In *Van Duyn* v *Home Office* (1974), the ECJ also identified that measures could be either vertically directly effective (where the measure could be used in an action against the state), or horizontally directly effective (where the measure could be enforced against another individual).

Directives can never be horizontally directly effective because they fail the non-dependent test in *Van Gend & Loos*. However, the ECJ in *Van Duyn* was prepared to overlook this limitation because 'it would be incompatible with the binding effect attributed to a Directive by [Article 249] to exclude, in principle, the possibility that the obligation which it imposes may be invoked by those concerned'.

As a result it has been held that a directive can be enforced provided the three criteria for direct effect are met but only where the time limit for implementation has passed, for example in *Pubblico Ministero* v *Ratti* (1979). In addition, a directive can be only directly effective vertically against the state and not horizontally against other individuals, as shown in *Marshall* v *Southampton and South West Hampshire AHA* (1984).

The concept of state has been extended to include an 'arm' of the state or 'emanation' of the state. An emanation of the state is determined according to the test in *Foster* v *British Gas plc* (1989) which states that the body must:
- provide a public service
- be under the control of the state
- exercise special powers over those enjoyed by private companies

This, of course, creates major anomalies in the case of private bodies — *Duke* v *GEC Reliance Ltd* (1988) — against whom an unimplemented directive cannot be enforced.

Indirect effect

As a result of the limitations of using vertical direct effect, the ECJ in *Von Colson and Kamann* v *Land Nordrhein-Westfalen* (1983) also created the concept of indirect effect.

Because there is an obligation on member states under Article 10 to conform with and give effect to EU law, irrespective of whether or not it is directly effective, then, according to the ECJ, national courts should interpret national law so as to give effect to the provisions in an improperly implemented directive.

State liability

Another way developed by the ECJ to avoid the problems of direct effect and directives came in *Francovich* v *Italy* (1990). The ECJ held that 'the full effectiveness of EC provisions…and the rights they recognise would be undermined if individuals were unable to recover damages where their rights were infringed by a breach of EC law attributable to a member state'.

The ECJ developed a test to determine when citizens should be able to sue the state for the effects of the non-implementation of a directive. The test has subsequently been developed in *Brasserie du Pecheur SA* v *Germany* (1996) and in *R* v *Secretary of State for Transport, ex parte Factortame* (1993). The conditions for liability are now:
- the measure must confer rights on individuals, the contents of which must be identifiable in the wording
- the breach by the member state must be sufficiently serious to justify imposing liability on the state
- there must be a causal link between the damage suffered and the breach of EU law by the member state

Generally it must be shown that the breach is sufficiently serious. However, the case of *Dillenkofer* v *Federal Republic of Germany* (1994) identified that non-implementation of a directive is always sufficiently serious to warrant state liability.

Article 234 references

The Article 234 reference procedure is critical to both supremacy and direct effect, because it is the means of ensuring the uniform application of the law throughout the member states. The procedure is the means by which national courts are guided on the 'meaning or validity' of EU law in a case which depends for its outcome on a correct interpretation of EU law.

A reference can be made by any court or tribunal (discretionary referral) but must be made by a court against which there is no further judicial remedy, for instance the final appeal court (mandatory referral).

A reference can only be made where EU law is relevant to the case and the interpretation is necessary to the outcome. The ECJ has developed the following test from the case of *CILFIT Srl* v *Ministro della Sanita* (1982) for courts to determine when a reference is not necessary:
- where EU law is irrelevant or only peripheral to the main issue
- where there is already an existing interpretation (here the principle of *acte clair* applies)

- where the correct interpretation is so obvious that the court should not be in any doubt

UK courts also drew up their own guidelines in *Bulmer* v *Bollinger* (1974). Before referring, the judge must be sure that:
- EU law would be conclusive of the case
- there is no previous ECJ ruling
- the doctrine of *acte clair* does not apply
- the facts of the case are already decided
- the delay caused by reference is not unwarranted

Law reform

Purpose of law reform

There are four key purposes of law reform:
1 to improve law
2 to update law, and make it more relevant
3 to rationalise law by consolidation
4 to make law more accessible

Impetus for law reform

Various bodies and groups provide the impetus for law reform:
- political parties, through their policies in their election manifestos
- royal commissions, e.g. the Taylor Report on football grounds (1989)
- pressure groups, of two types:
  - interest groups, which advance the interests of a particular group of people, e.g. trade unions
  - cause groups, which further a particular cause, e.g. Shelter campaigning on homelessness

Law reform agencies

There are a number of bodies that have responsibility for law reform in the English legal system. They ensure that the law is kept under review and make suggestions regarding the development of the law.

The Law Commission

The Law Commission was created by Parliament by the **Law Commissions Act 1965**.

It is the only full-time law reform body and its role is to keep the law under review. It has a key role in the codification, consolidation and repeal of the law. It is a permanent body staffed by lawyers of high standing, with a High Court judge as its chairman.

It can decide its own areas of law to research and review but the government can also direct it to research particular areas. Examples of changes to the law resulting from its work are the **Unfair Contract Terms Act 1977** and the **Occupiers Liability Act 1984**.

Key problems of the Law Commission are that ministers have demanded that it researches irrelevant matters, and also it has had a poor success rate regarding the implementation of its work.

The Criminal Law Revision Committee

The Criminal Law Revision Committee was created in 1957, originally as a tool of the Home Secretary. It is an *ad hoc* body, also now used by the Lord Chancellor. This part-time body's focus is the criminal law. It last sat in 1986.

It originally suggested the end to the right of silence as early as 1972. Its greatest success was the **Theft Act 1968**.

The Law Reform Committee

The Law Reform Committee was created in 1952 and used by the Lord Chancellor. It is a part-time body focused on civil rather than criminal law, and is less controversial than the Criminal Law Revision Committee. It is still an *ad hoc* body and so it is subject to the demands of its creator. A key success of its work is the **Latent Damages Act 1986**.

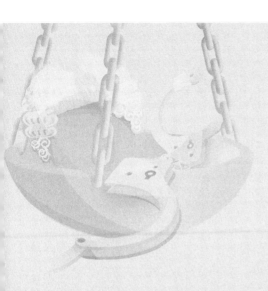

Questions
&
Answers

This section provides you with four source-based questions from the four main areas of Unit G152 covered in this guide in the style that you will find in the exam. Each question is broken down into three parts. As explained in the introduction, part (a) and part (b) questions are worth 15 marks each and part (c) questions are worth 30 marks. The total mark available for the paper is therefore 60.

A-, C- and E-grade answers are provided for each question. The A-grade answers should give you a clear idea of the approach and structure required. The C-grade answers have been included to illustrate some of the common problems that result in students achieving lower marks. You will see that E-grade answers are often unbalanced and tend to pass on the basis of one good answer from the three parts.

You should not take the A-grade responses as being model answers for you to learn off by heart because the sources and the questions in the exam will be different from those presented here. Instead, you should try to give your own answers to the questions first and then compare them with the answers here to see what you are doing well and where you can make improvements. You will also be able to learn some of the common weaknesses and mistakes made by candidates, by reading the C- and E-grade answers and the examiner's comments after them so that you ensure that you do not make the same mistakes or that you give fuller answers in the exam to get a better grade.

At the end of each of the four questions and answers there is a section entitled 'Additional examiner comment'. This gives you clear guidance in each case of how to use the information that is provided in the source materials and also the information that you should be bringing to the answer that you cannot find from the sources themselves. This section gives you the means of improving your answer and therefore your grade.

Examiner's comments

Each answer is accompanied by examiner's comments, preceded by the icon ℮. These indicate where credit has been given, recognising the candidate's use of the examinable skills, as explained in the introduction. Part (a) questions are intended to test AO1 skills of recall of knowledge, part (b) questions focus on the AO2 skill of application, and part (c) questions test knowledge and evaluation and analysis. Part (i), testing knowledge, is worth 15 marks. Part (ii), testing analysis and evaluation, is worth 12 AO2 marks and 3 AO3 marks. In the C- and E-grade answers, the examiner indicates possible improvements that could be made to achieve a higher grade.

Remember also the AO3 objective which calls for effective communication skills, use of appropriate legal terminology and correct spelling, punctuation and grammar.

Doctrine of precedent

In *Shivpuri* (1986), the House of Lords overruled its own precedent from *Anderton* v *Ryan* (1985) from only the previous year. It did so in order to correct an error of interpretation of the Criminal Attempts Act 1981 on attempting the impossible. In overruling the case the House of Lords made use of the Practice Statement 1966 which allows the
5 court to depart from past precedent 'when it appears right to do so'. Lord Bridge explained that the House was bound to depart from the previous case because there was no basis on which to distinguish the two cases on the material facts.

Prior to 1966, the House of Lords was bound by its own past precedents from the decision in *London Tramways* v *London CC* (1898) — distinguishing, which is available to all
10 courts, being one of the only ways available to avoid past precedents. The Practice Statement allows the House of Lords to develop the law and avoid injustice, but this flexibility is only available to the House of Lords.

Shivpuri was the first use of the Practice Statement in criminal law. The Practice Statement did identify the need for certainty in criminal law, so it is not surprising that
15 it was 20 years before the House chose to apply it in this context. In any case, the House of Lords has shown reluctance in using the powers given in the Practice Statement.

(a) The source refers to the process of distinguishing (lines 7 and 9).
Using the source and other cases describe this process. (12 marks + 3 marks)

(b) Using the information in the source, consider whether the earlier
cases could be overruled in each of the following situations:
  (i) The House of Lords in a 1961 case, wishes to overrule a
House of Lords case from 1950 which it believes will cause
injustice if applied in the 1961 case.
  (ii) The House of Lords in a 1987 case wishes to overrule a
House of Lords case from 1921 which it believes is now outdated.
  (iii) The Court of Appeal in a 2004 case wishes to overrule a Court
of Appeal case from 1967 which it believes will cause injustice
in the 2004 case if applied. (15 marks)

(c) (i) Using the source and other cases, explain how the Practice
Statement works. (15 marks)
  (ii) Discuss the extent to which 'the House of Lords has shown
reluctance in using the powers given in the Practice
Statement'. (12 marks + 3 marks)

■ ■ ■

question

A-grade answer

(a) Distinguishing is when cases are separated or taken as being different from each other. The court looks at the facts of the two cases to decide whether they are similar enough for the precedent in one case to be followed in the other, meaning that the outcome will then be the same as in the previous case. However, if enough significant differences are found, then the courts will distinguish them and there will be a different outcome. Two cases which illustrate the process of distinguishing are *Balfour* v *Balfour* and *Merritt* v *Merritt*. In *Balfour* v *Balfour* the wife was told by doctors that she should stay in England while her husband went to work in Ceylon. When he went, Mr Balfour promised that he would pay his wife an allowance, but they later separated and he stopped paying her. Mrs Balfour still wanted her allowance and sued. The court decided that there was no intention to create legal relations because it was a domestic arrangement. In the case of *Merritt* v *Merritt*, however, the couple agreed upon the husband paying the mortgage in his wife's name, but they were already estranged when the agreement was made. The court distinguished the two cases and said that if the couple had still been together when the agreement was made, then they would have followed *Balfour*, but due to them already being apart the court said that there was intention to create legal relations as this did not count as a domestic arrangement in the circumstances. This is totally different to *Shivpuri* and *Anderton* v *Ryan* in the source, where, because the court could find no distinguishing features, it was possible instead to depart from the precedent using the Practice Statement.

> This is a very good answer. Distinguishing is clearly defined from the start. Appropriate case law is used in detail to illustrate the process effectively. There is also reference back to the source, where the word 'distinguishing' is used, and a further explanation is given which supplements what goes before.

(b) (i) The House of Lords in the 1961 case would still have to follow the precedent set by the 1950 case, even if it did lead to injustice. This is because even though the House of Lords knew that this was a wrong precedent to follow, the Practice Statement only came into force in 1966 and it would not have existed at the time of this scenario. Therefore, the House of Lords could not depart from the precedent it set in 1950. It could only distinguish if the facts were different.

(ii) This case is different. The 1987 case comes after the Practice Statement was introduced, so the House of Lords could depart from the precedent it set in the 1921 case. The Practice Statement gave the House of Lords the right to change precedent in order to develop the law, so it would be able to depart from the past precedent which it thinks is outdated.

(iii) The Court of Appeal does not have the Practice Statement, so it could not change the precedent in the 1967 case.

> A good answer. The answers to both (i) and (ii) are comprehensive, including not only understanding of the availability of the Practice Statement because of the

dates involved but also the purposes for which it can be used. In (i) there is also the reference to distinguishing. (iii) is correct but might have been taken further, as (i) was, by adding 'unless any of the exceptions in *Young* v *Bristol Aeroplane* apply'.

(c) (i) Before 1966 the House of Lords was bound by its own past precedents because of the case of *London Tramways* v *London County Council*. It could only avoid past precedent if it could distinguish the case or if the past case was decided *per incuriam*, which means in error. As it says in the source, the Practice Statement allows the House of Lords to depart from past precedent 'when it appears right to do so'. As it also says in the source, this will be when it prevents injustice or helps to develop the law.

The House of Lords first used the Practice Statement in *Conway* v *Rimmer* on a technical matter. In *Herrington* v *British Railways Board* the House of Lords used the Practice Statement to overrule *Addie* v *Dumbreck* on the duty of care owed to child trespassers. The Practice Statement was first used in a criminal case, *Shivpuri*, to overrule *Anderton* v *Ryan* on impossible attempts, to come into line with statute. The Practice Statement is only available to the House of Lords and recognises that there is a need to maintain certainty in the law

(ii) The House of Lords does not often use the Practice Statement, even though it has the opportunity to, so this shows its reluctance. Sometimes it will not use it even though it thinks that injustice will be caused or even if it thinks the law is wrong. In *Jones* v *Secretary of State* all of the judges thought that it would cause injustice if *Re Dowling* were followed, and four of the five judges thought the case had been decided wrongly, but they still would not change the precedent. The first use of the Practice Statement in *Conway* v *Rimmer* was only on a technical matter so it did not really develop the law. The first use in a civil case in *Herrington* v *British Railways Board*, which overruled *Addie* v *Dumbreck*, allowed that there was a duty of care owed to child trespassers. This helped prevent injustice because young children would not be aware of the dangers of trespassing on the railway.

In *Milliangos* the Practice Statement was used too to overrule *Havana Railways* and allowed damages to be paid in a different currency from sterling. At the time of *Havana* the precedent was good, as sterling was a powerful currency. However, when the case of *Schorsch Meier* went to the Court of Appeal, it was seen that sterling was no longer a powerful currency and so it gave the judgement in the currency the claimants wanted. This was seen by the lawyers in *Milliangos*, so they asked for it too and the case was then appealed to the House of Lords, which changed the decision in *Havana* as it was evident that times had changed.

The first use of the Practice Statement in a criminal case in *Shivpuri*, which overruled *Anderton* v *Ryan*, was 20 years after the Practice Statement was made, as can be seen from the source. It shows that the House of Lords was even more reluctant to use the Practice Statement in criminal cases, although this may be because the Practice Statement said that it had to maintain certainty in criminal

law. The case was not really about developing the law or preventing injustice as it was just because the House of Lords had made a mistake in *Anderton* v *Ryan* in interpreting the Criminal Attempts Act.

The rule of *stare decisis* plays a vital role in why the House of Lords is reluctant to change past precedents. The rule means to stand by your decisions and allows the law to have a degree of certainty. If there were no need for certainty, the House of Lords might be more willing to depart. The Practice Statement has given the House of Lords a great deal of flexibility, but it does not often use it, showing that there is reluctance to use it.

> This is quite a comprehensive account of the Practice Statement for an AS answer, with an extensive use of cases and good focus on the questions asked. Good use has also been made of the information given in the source. The candidate has shown some of the problems arising before the introduction of the Practice Statement, highlighting its significance. Another good aspect of the answer is that there is a conclusion for (ii).

■ ■ ■

C-grade answer

(a) Distinguishing is when a judge in a case decides that he does not want to be bound by an earlier case so he will distinguish between the present case and the past case and find that the material facts are different so that he can distinguish between them and not have to follow the past case. An example of distinguishing is *Balfour* v *Balfour* and *Merritt* v *Merritt*.

> The candidate shows a reasonably clear understanding of how the process of distinguishing works and there is a useful comment on why judges may want to distinguish. Appropriate case law is included. If this had been developed, it would have enhanced the answer and secured more marks.

(b) (i) The Practice Statement was not introduced until 1966. Before that time the House of Lords was bound by its own past precedent.

(ii) The Practice Statement was introduced in 1966 after which the House of Lords was able to depart from its past precedents when it appears right to do so.

(iii) The Court of Appeal does not have the Practice Statement so it has to follow its past precedents unless *Young* v *Bristol Aeroplane* applies.

> All three answers are correct as far as they go. The candidate clearly understands the issues that are being raised but loses out on the higher marks because the principles are not applied to the scenarios.

(c) (i) The Practice Statement allows the House of Lords to overrule past precedent if it believes that the past precedent was wrong or if it would cause injustice or if it were outdated.

Shivpuri was the first criminal case where the Practice Statement was used to overrule a previous wrong decision. In *Anderton* v *Ryan*, the defendant was previously found not guilty of attempt in 1985 for buying what she thought were stolen goods but it could not be proved that they were stolen. In 1986, only 1 year after, Shivpuri was charged with smuggling drugs into the country. In fact, it was only vegetable matter even though Shivpuri really believed that he was carrying drugs. The court realised that the intent to do so should be punished and so Shivpuri had to be convicted for attempting the impossible so it went against its precedent in *Anderton* v *Ryan*. This was because the court believed that the earlier case had been decided wrongly and that it had got the law wrong. Another example of this was *R* v *G & R* which got rid of *Caldwell* recklessness because the court felt that recklessness should always be subjective.

Another reason for which the Practice Statement has been used is where the past law is out of date or unjust. This was shown in *Herrington* v *British Railways* which overruled *Addie* v *Dumbreck*. This case concluded that there should be greater liability to children and this was because attitudes to child safety were different from the earlier case.

(ii) Lord Denning argued for many years that the Practice Statement should be given to the Court of Appeal too. This was because fewer cases go to the House of Lords and some people cannot afford to go to the House of Lords and so some aspects of the law could be wrong for a long time. However, the law needs to have certainty. The Practice Statement allows the House of Lords some flexibility but it is hard for people to know how to abide by the law if it is not certain and also for lawyers to know how to advise their clients on the outcome of cases. This is why the Practice Statement powers have been restricted to the House of Lords only.

✑ These are quite good answers in respect of the AO1 material. Knowledge is shown over and above that given in the source, including some up-to-date information, and it is reasonably clear and comprehensive. There is some comment but the answers lack focus on the questions set and there is little in (ii) on the reluctance or otherwise of the House of Lords to use the Practice Statement, so the candidate would not pick up many AO2 marks.

■ ■ ■

E-grade answer

(a) Distinguishing is only binding on cases that have the same points of law and similar facts. It is used by judges to avoid a decision from a previous case which would usually be binding in practice.

✑ This is a very limited answer. The candidate has made a valid but limited point in the second sentence and has not really defined distinguishing, nor made reference to any cases. This answer would be short of a pass mark.

question

(b) (i) The House of Lords was bound by its own decisions after the case of *London Street Tramways* v *London County Council* (1898) in which it decided this because of the importance of certainty in the law. Then the Practice Statement was introduced in 1966 by the Lord Chancellor and it stated that the House of Lords would normally treat itself as bound by its own decisions but it could depart from them when it appeared right to do so. Therefore in the 1961 case the House of Lords could not overrule the 1950 case as it would be bound by its own past decisions because the case is before the Practice Statement was made.

(ii) Due to the Practice Statement being made in 1966, the House of Lords could depart from its past decisions when it appeared right to do so. Because the case here is after the Practice Statement came in, the House of Lords can change the 1921 case.

(iii) The Court of Appeal cannot change its past decisions unless it can use one of the exceptions in *Young* v *Bristol Aeroplane*. The first is where there are two conflicting decisions, when the Court of Appeal will decide which one to follow and which one to overrule. The second exception is where a previous decision must be overruled if it conflicts with a House of Lords decision. The third exception is where the case was decided *per incuriam*, which means carelessly or by mistake. In the Criminal Division, precedent is not followed so strictly because a person's liberty is at stake.

📝 This is generally well answered. The candidate has shown a full understanding of the powers of the House of Lords before and after the Practice Statement and applied that accurately to the scenarios in (i) and (ii). The answer given for (iii) lets the candidate down. He/she clearly had enough understanding to gain maximum marks and gave full detail on the powers of the Court of Appeal but then forgot to apply them to the scenario.

(c) (i) The Practice Statement was formed by Lord Chancellor Gardiner in 1966. He stated that the House of Lords could change its past decisions if it appears right to do so. In *Shivpuri* the House of Lords used the Practice Statement to overrule *Anderton* v *Ryan*.

(ii) Lord Denning thought that this was a bad idea as the Practice Statement only applies to the House of Lords and not to the Court of Appeal. When it appears right to change the law could also be different for each judge.

📝 These are very limited answers, particularly for a question carrying half the marks. The candidate has taken from the source when the Practice Statement will be used, but with no development and omitting to state the grounds for using it which are given in the second paragraph of the source. *Shivpuri* overruling *Anderton* v *Ryan* is recited from the source again without any development to show understanding. There is some minimal AO2 credit in (ii) for the comment on Lord Denning's attitudes, although this is off the point of discussion called for in the question. Overall the candidate would not get a pass mark for this answer.

This is a classic example of an E-grade answer. The candidate has secured very limited marks for both (a) and (c), borrowing mostly from the source and displaying little extra knowledge, but has secured a pass overall with some good application in part (b).

Additional examiner comment

Source-based papers provide you with information that helps you to answer the questions set. The questions also refer to the sources so that they are asking you to respond to the information provided in the source. The best way to achieve the highest marks is to make the most of all information that can be found in the source. Stronger candidates can find clues in the source that aid their memory and weaker candidates can easily pull their marks up. Of course, not everything that you could write on the topic is in the source, but you can use the information that is there to remind you of the extra information that you can bring to your answer.

If you spend a few moments at the beginning of the exam highlighting all the useful information in the source, you will actually save yourself time in the long run. More importantly you will not miss anything in the source that you can use in your answer. You might also like to add the letter (a) or (b) or (c) in the margin next to your highlighting and you can then refer to it quickly when you are writing, without having to read through the whole source again.

In the source above there is lots of information that you can use to good effect. Below is an outline of what you can use from the source for each part of the question as well as other information not in the source but which the examiner would expect to see in a good candidate's script.

Part (a)
Information you can find in the source
In the second paragraph of the source there is a reference to distinguishing. It explains that it is available to all courts and also that it is one way of avoiding past precedents.

At the end of the first paragraph there is an explanation of why distinguishing could not be used in *Shivpuri*, because the material facts were so similar to the case of *Anderton* v *Ryan*. This is a reminder of how distinguishing works. Even by just using common sense you ought to be able to attempt a definition.

Extra information you should give in your answer
- A proper definition — that courts can distinguish when the material facts of the cases are essentially different so that the principle in the first case cannot be applied to the later case.
- Cases that illustrate how distinguishing works — classic favourites among students include *Balfour* v *Balfour* and *Merritt* v *Merritt*, and *Rylands* v *Fletcher* and *Read* v *Lyons*. As long as they explain the point it does not matter which cases you use, but you will not achieve the high-level marks without mentioning some.

Part (b)

Information you can find in the source

Application questions are all about using the information in the source and applying it to factual situations given in the questions, so you cannot really answer part (b) without using the source.

Here, the critical information can be found in the first sentence of the second paragraph: the date of the Practice Statement and the fact that before 1966 the House of Lords was bound by its own past precedents just like the other courts.

Looking at the factual situations in the questions, there is another big clue to be found in the last sentence of the second paragraph — the fact that the Practice Statement is only available to the House of Lords and no other court.

Extra information you should give in your answer

Your task is to apply the above information to the individual questions.

In (i) the cases involve the House of Lords, and the years 1950 and 1961 both come before the Practice Statement so that the past precedent could not be changed. You might also remember that the House of Lords could distinguish if the facts of the two cases were sufficiently different, or overrule where the previous precedent was decided *per incuriam* or where it was inconsistent with later statute law. However, there are not enough facts in the scenario to say whether any of these would be possible.

In (ii) the cases again involve the House of Lords and the later case comes after the Practice Statement, so it could be used to overrule the former case. You might also spot that the reason the House wants to change the past rule is one of the justifications given in the Practice Statement, to develop the law by removing outdated law, so overruling would be appropriate.

In the case of (iii) you should be able to spot that the dates of the two cases are irrelevant because they involve the Court of Appeal which does not have the powers given in the Practice Statement. You might also be able to remember that the Court of Appeal could still avoid the past precedent if it could distinguish or if any of the exceptions in *Young* v *Bristol Aeroplane* apply, although there are insufficient facts in the scenario to say that this would be the case.

Part (c)

Information you can find in the source

- In the first paragraph you are told that the Practice Statement can be used 'when it appears right to do so' and in the second paragraph when this will be — 'to develop the law and avoid injustice'.
- In the first paragraph you also have the example of cases using the Practice Statement, *Shivpuri* overruling *Anderton* v *Ryan*, along with some important facts and why it was used.
- In the second paragraph you are given the previous rule from *London Tramways* and one of the only ways at that time of avoiding past precedents — distinguishing.
- In the third paragraph you are not only told that the House of Lords has been reluctant to use the powers of the Practice Statement but you are also given an example — not using it in criminal law for 20 years.

Extra information you should give in your answer

The most important additional information for (i) is extra cases for AO1 and for (ii) is examples of reluctance, or indeed willingness, to use the Practice Statement for AO2.

There are several cases you could use: *Conway* v *Rimmer* (1968) and *Duncan* v *Cammell Laird* (1942); *Herrington* v *British Railways Board* (1972) and *Addie* v *Dumbreck* (1929); *Howe* (1987) and *Lynch* (1975); *Jones* v *Secretary of State for Social Services* (1972) and *Re Dowling* (1967) and others, including the recent case of *R* v *G & R* (2003) overruling *Caldwell* (1982) which had been criticised for years.

For good AO2 marks you could identify:

- the few times the Practice Statement has been used
- that *Conway* v *Rimmer*, the first use, only involved a technical point
- that the first civil use was after 6 years in *Herrington*
- that the first criminal use was 20 years later in *Shivpuri*, but even then only to correct an error the House had made the previous year (information supplied in the source)
- that it was not used in *Jones,* even though all of the judges thought that applying *Dowling* would lead to injustice and four of them felt that *Dowling*, in any case, was wrongly decided
- that the House might never have had the opportunity to overrule the outdated rule in *Havana Railways* in *Milliangos* if the Court of Appeal had not gone against the rules of precedent in *Schorsch Meier*

Legislation

An Act of Parliament becomes law only after a bill has passed through various stages in Parliament in both the House of Commons and the House of Lords. The final stage is where the monarch gives approval to the bill.

Delegated legislation, on the other hand, is made by a person or a body other than Par-
5 liament but with the authority of Parliament. This authority is often granted in an 'enabling' Act which sets out the general framework of the law and then allows the other body to provide the essential detail. There are three types of delegated legislation: statutory instruments which are introduced by government departments; Orders in Council passed by the Privy Council; and bylaws made usually by local authorities.

10 Delegated legislation is often preferred because of the length of time that it takes to pass an Act of Parliament and the inability of Parliament to act quickly in times of emergency. Delegated legislation is criticised, however, because it is undemocratic and made by non-elected people. This would be satisfactory if there were adequate controls.

15 Some control is exercised by Parliament and some by the courts, but in reality effective supervision is difficult. The public are often unaware of the existence of delegated legislation and also of the means of challenging it. Some statutory instruments are sub-ject to the affirmative resolution procedure which ensures that parliamentary attention is drawn to them, but it is rarely possible to prevent the delegated legislation from being
20 passed. There is also a Scrutiny Committee, but it can only report back its findings and lacks power to alter statutory instruments. The courts have some control too through the process of judicial review, but this relies on individuals successfully challenging the delegated legislation in the courts.

(a) The source (lines 1–3) refers to the stages by which a bill becomes an Act of Parliament. Briefly describe these stages.   (12 marks + 3 marks)

(b) Identify and explain which type of delegated legislation would be most appropriate in the following situations:
   (i) A town council wishes to impose parking restrictions in a busy high street.
   (ii) A minister needs to introduce new regulations following an Act on social security benefits.
   (iii) There is a need to introduce some emergency powers in time of war.   (15 marks)

(c) (i) Using the source and other examples, describe the controls on delegated legislation.   (15 marks)
   (ii) Discuss the advantages and disadvantages of delegated legislation.   (12 marks + 3 marks)

A-grade answer

(a) A bill can start in either parliamentary House, the House of Commons or the House of Lords, although most usually start in the House of Commons.

In the first reading the title of the bill and its main aims are read out. The second reading is more detailed. All aspects of the bill are considered and debated before a vote is taken. All of the MPs leave the room and go through two different doors to show how they are voting. If the bill passes at this stage, then it goes on to what is called the committee stage. This is where a small group of MPs is chosen to be part of a standing committee. The committee goes through the bill clause by clause and tries to spot any mistakes or problems. Once this is done there is a report stage where the committee reports back to the House and suggests any changes that it thinks are needed. There is then a third reading and the House has to agree on the bill and any amendments to it.

If the bill passes all of these stages, it is passed to the House of Lords where it goes through the same stages. If the House of Lords refuses to pass the bill, it can be introduced again at the next parliamentary session. The bill does not actually need the House of Lords' consent and eventually can become an Act without it.

The bill then has to have the royal assent. The queen must give her approval before the bill is enacted. In fact this is always given. After the royal assent, the bill comes into force at midnight of the same day, unless another date has been set. Some Acts take a long time to come into force.

🖉 This is a clear and comprehensive answer. There is even some extra detail that would not have been expected or demanded by the examiner, for instance the comment about the inability of the House of Lords to prevent a bill from eventually becoming law.

(b) (i) The parking restrictions would be introduced as a bylaw. There is no requirement for Parliament to debate and pass laws on local parking restrictions. It is a law of local interest and for this reason Parliament has delegated the power to local councils to introduce it. A statutory instrument would cover the whole country, so it would be inappropriate for local matters. In this case there is no emergency, so an Order in Council would also be inappropriate.

(ii) The best type of delegated legislation to introduce regulations already outlined in an enabling Act would be a statutory instrument. The people working for the ministry would have the expertise to know what sort of regulation is needed and, in any case, the Act would have set out the broad principles; it is the specific rules that the statutory instrument would be concerned with.

(iii) When there is an emergency and in times of war, Orders in Council are used to introduce the powers that are needed. This would enable the government to pass the legislation quickly, as trying to pass an Act would take far too long. This delegated legislation would be introduced by the Privy Council.

All three answers are detailed. The candidate shows clear understanding not just of which type of delegated legislation would be chosen and why, but also of wider issues.

(c) (i) Delegated legislation is controlled in two ways: one by Parliament and the other by the courts. Bills can be subject to an affirmative resolution procedure. This means that Parliament debates and votes on the bill in the normal way, and so it is an effective control. However, this procedure is rarely used. Most delegated legislation is introduced by negative resolution, where it is merely left in a lobby in Parliament for MPs to review and to raise objections if they have any. Under the negative resolution procedure, there is only a period of 40 days available in which to raise objections, so it is a much less effective control. Parliament has a scrutiny committee. This reports its findings back to Parliament, but it cannot alter statutory instruments.

The courts have some control through judicial review, which is when the court decides whether the delegated legislation is *ultra vires*, meaning beyond its powers, but this depends on someone challenging the delegated legislation in the courts, and it is therefore not very effective.

(ii) There are many advantages to having delegated legislation. First, it saves time for Parliament, which would have to debate and vote on every issue. There are many more statutory instruments introduced in a year than Acts, so Parliament does not have the time to look at all of these. Delegated legislation allows Parliament to set out the framework of the law in an enabling Act and then the detail is added in by the other body. Parliament does not have all of the knowledge to introduce all laws and with delegated legislation experts can be used to draft the legislation in the specific areas. Parliament cannot act quickly enough in emergencies, so Orders in Council can be used to get the law through more quickly, for example during wars. Parliament also does not have local knowledge and it would waste a lot of time if it had to pass laws to deal with local problems, so local councils are given the power to make minor local laws. Delegated legislation can also be changed more quickly than an Act.

Delegated legislation has many disadvantages, however. It is undemocratic and made by unelected people. There is a lot of it, so it is hard to keep up with what the law is, and since it is not widely publicised the public does not always know that there are new regulations on something and this can be seen as unfair. Delegated legislation is made by experts in particular fields, meaning that it may not be easy to understand. The controls are also not very effective. The Scrutiny Committee can only report back. Since only a few statutory instruments use the affirmative resolution, most of it is not voted on. Judicial review is also not very effective because it depends on people being able to bring an action in the court.

Much in these answers has made use of the material in the source and some of it could obviously have been developed more, e.g. discussion in (i) of the scrutiny committee and the process of judicial review for AO1 and in (ii) of the disadvantages for AO2. However, the source is not merely copied; some thought has been given to it and it has been used effectively. In addition, there is information that is not in the source which shows a wider knowledge and understanding. Possibly the reference in the source to the affirmative resolution has prompted the candidate to think of the negative resolution procedure, but these are both clearly understood. The reference to and explanation of *ultra vires* shows that the candidate knows what judicial review is about. Besides this, there is a well-rehearsed list of advantages and disadvantages, some developed better than others.

■ ■ ■

C-grade answer

(a) Acts of Parliament pass through many stages before they become law. The first stage is the first reading and this is when the bill is read out to Parliament. The second stage is the second reading, which is where the proposed Act is looked at in more detail. The third stage is where the proposed Act is revised or amended if necessary. The fourth stage is a report stage where all the amendments are taken into account. The fifth stage is the House of Lords stage. Sometimes the House of Lords opposes the Act and sends it back to Parliament. The final stage is the royal assent, which is the signature of the queen. It has been many years since a king or queen has not given royal assent.

The major stages are generally understood and there is some detail in parts. The committee stage is not named, although the basic elements of that stage are shown in the answer. The third reading is also omitted and there is no reference to the fact that the House of Lords follows the same stages, with mention only that the bill is passed on to it. Nevertheless, overall the candidate demonstrates some good understanding.

(b) (i) To introduce parking restrictions, we would need to use a bylaw. This is because local councils introduce bylaws.

(ii) To introduce legislation regarding the implementation of regulations outlined in an enabling Act, we would need to use a statutory instrument. This is because the minister would know what was in the enabling Act.

(iii) To introduce emergency measures during a war, we would need to look at Orders in Council. This is because to pass an Act would not be quick enough.

The candidate gives correct but quite limited answers to all three parts. The explanations are somewhat unsophisticated and the candidate could have added more detail throughout.

(c) (i) There are two types of controls of delegated legislation: one is parliamentary and the other is through the courts. Affirmative resolutions are a good way of controlling delegated legislation because then Parliament has to debate it and vote on it. However, this is only used for important things and most is introduced by negative resolution when the delegated legislation is merely left in

question

Parliament and MPs raise objections if they have any. Negative resolution is much more difficult to control, as even if an MP spots something wrong with it he/she only has 40 days to bring it to Parliament's attention which, with the limited time, would be difficult. There is also a Scrutiny Committee which reports its findings back to Parliament, but it cannot alter statutory instruments. It is also possible to challenge delegated legislation in the courts through judicial review. However, not many people are aware of what delegated legislation is and so they might not know what the laws are and they are even less likely to know how to challenge such legislation.

(ii) Delegated legislation has advantages over Acts of Parliament because it can be made quicker and Parliament does not have to debate it all. The minister can look at the enabling Act and his department can then produce the rules that are needed to fill in the detail that is not in the Act itself. It can also be introduced in times of emergency, as with Orders in Council, and it can be used to make laws that are useful in a particular town, as with bylaws. The disadvantage is that it is undemocratic and made by unelected people, and also the controls are not very effective.

There is not the degree of detail in (i) that would be expected of an A-grade answer and much of it is borrowed from the source, although the comment on the 'negative resolution' procedure shows some good knowledge and understanding. In (ii) the AO2 again is not very developed, although the candidate makes maximum use of the help that is given in the source and does develop that to some extent.

■ ■ ■

E-grade answer

(a) Acts of Parliament have to go through different stages before they become an Act. First, the bill has to go before the House of Commons. Here, there is a first reading when the bill is read out. Then there is a second reading where the bill is debated and voted on. Then amendments are added to the bill in a committee. These amendments are reported to the House by the committee and they are debated. Then there is a third reading and a vote is taken whether to accept the law. Then the House of Lords looks at the bill too. Then the queen has to give her signature which is called royal assent. Then the Act becomes law.

This is a reasonable answer. The candidate understands the whole process and in parts has given some good detail. More could have been made of the House of Lords, but there is still enough understanding shown for a good mark. The style could be improved, for instance by avoiding the repetitive use of 'Then'.

(b) (i) Parking restrictions would have to be made in a statutory instrument by the minister responsible for the roads.

(ii) The implementation of regulations outlined in an enabling Act would need to be made in a statutory instrument to follow the rules in the enabling Act.

(iii) The emergency powers in a time of war would need to be made in an Order in Council.

🖉 The answer to (i) is plainly wrong. The answers to (ii) and (iii) are correct, although there is little in the way of explanation and so high marks could not be given.

(c) (i) 'Some control is exercised by Parliament and some by the courts, but in reality effective supervision is difficult' is a fair statement because the public is often unaware of the existence of delegated legislation and also of the means of challenging it. Parliament has the affirmative resolution procedure and the Scrutiny Committee, and the courts have some control through the process of judicial review, but this is not really enough.

(ii) The advantage of delegated legislation is that there are some controls, but the disadvantage is that the controls aren't very effective.

🖉 Overall, this is a typically unbalanced answer of the type common to E-grade responses. The candidate has done little of credit for the most important part (c), has provided acceptable answers on two out of three parts of (b), but would manage to get a pass because of a good answer to part (a). The candidate was clearly more confident and had more knowledge of the basic process of legislation than of delegated legislation.

Additional examiner comment

Go back to Question 1 and read the first two paragraphs in the 'Additional examiner comment'. Here you will find the advantages of source-based questions and some important points on preparing your answer in the exam.

In the source above there is lots of information that you might use to good effect. Below is an outline of what you can use from the source for each part of the question as well as other information not in the source but which the examiner would hope to see in a good script.

Part (a)
Information you can find in the source
In the first paragraph of the source you are told that there are stages in both the House of Commons and the House of Lords and also that the final stage is where the monarch gives approval.

Extra information you should give in your answer
You have been given a good start in the source but not the detail, and this is what you need to add. Remember the command words say 'briefly describe', so you need some detail but not elaborate detail. You would need to identify the five stages in the House of Commons that are then repeated in the House of Lords and add a little detail showing your understanding:

- first reading — bill introduced
- second reading — debate plus vote
- committee stage — a committee looks at the bill in more detail and adds necessary amendments

- report stage — amendments suggested by committee reported back to Parliament
- third reading — final vote on bill

You should also be able to identify that the monarch's approval is called royal assent and that in modern times it is, in effect, a formality.

Part (b)

Information you can find in the source

Application questions are all about using the information in the source and applying it to factual situations given in the questions, so you cannot really answer part (b) without using the source.

The second paragraph identifies the three types of delegated legislation and what body makes them:

- statutory instruments — government departments
- Orders in Council — the Privy Council
- bylaws — local authorities, among others

Extra information you should give in your answer

Your task is to apply the above information to the individual questions and here you need to have a good understanding of the context in which the different types of delegated legislation operate.

(i) involves a town council wanting to introduce regulations on parking. The term 'town council' should be a significant clue, but you should be able to work out that parking restrictions in a specific high street is a local issue which would not require a national law in order to resolve it. You ought then to conclude, on the basis of similar reasoning, that the appropriate type of delegated legislation in this case is a bylaw.

(ii) involves a government minister wishing to introduce regulations that follow from an Act on social security benefits. Again, the word 'minister' is a big clue and you ought to be thinking of national law. An even bigger clue is that the regulations are to put in place principles in an enabling Act. You should be able to conclude that in this case the appropriate form of delegated legislation is a statutory instrument.

(iii) concerns emergency measures in time of war. You should remember that speedy action is one of the justifications for delegated legislation. You ought to know that it is the Privy Council that responds in similar situations through Orders in Council.

Part (c)

Information you can find in the source

The fourth paragraph contains a lot of useful information about the controls on delegated legislation:

- the reference to the affirmative resolution procedure
- the reference to the Scrutiny Committee and some detail on how it works
- the reference to judicial review

The second paragraph suggests the advantage that a general framework can be laid out in an Act with the detail then added by delegated legislation. Other advantages are given in the third paragraph, i.e. that delegated legislation is quicker than Acts and that it allows for a quick response in an emergency.

A disadvantage of delegated legislation is given in the third paragraph, i.e. that delegated legislation is undemocratic and made by unelected people. The fourth paragraph also states the disadvantage that the controls are ineffective, with the Scrutiny Committee, for instance, having no power to change delegated legislation.

Extra information you should give in your answer

For (i) the important additional AO1 information is extra detail on the controls, so you might contrast the affirmative resolution procedure with the negative resolution procedure where there is no scrutiny. You might also add more about the Scrutiny Committee itself. You should explain judicial review, that the Divisional Court of the Queen's Bench Division has the power to scrutinise decisions made by administrative bodies where a public law issue is involved, and that delegated legislation concerns acts that are *ultra vires* (beyond the powers of that body) and breaches of the rules of natural justice, for example lack of a fair hearing.

In (ii), for AO2 on advantages you might include that delegated legislation:

- saves parliamentary time
- allows for input by experts
- allows for individual laws on purely local issues

For AO2 on disadvantages you might include:

- more detail on the ineffectiveness of the controls
- the lack of publicity — people do not know about it
- the amount of delegated legislation

Statutory interpretation

The case of *R* v *Maginnis* (1987) *HL* was concerned with the interpretation of the Misuse of Drugs Act 1971, by s. 5(3) of which: 'it is an offence for a person to have a controlled drug in his possession, whether lawfully or not, with intent to supply it to another'.

5 Police had found a package of cannabis resin in the defendant's car. He said that the package was not his but had been left in his car by a friend for collection later. The defendant was convicted and appealed.

The House of Lords held that the defendant was guilty of the offence because a person in unlawful possession of a controlled drug left with him for safekeeping by another person had the necessary 'intent to supply it to another' (even though the supply was 10 not being made from the provider's own resources) if his intention was to return it to the other person and for that other person's purposes.

The majority of their Lordships claimed to apply the ordinary, natural meaning (the literal meaning) of the word 'supply'. Lord Goff of Chieveley, however, dissented on that very point and referred to definitions of the word given in the *Shorter Oxford English* 15 *Dictionary* (an extrinsic aid). In his view the word 'supply' was not appropriate to describe a transaction in which A handed back to B goods which B had previously left with A. Thus the cloakroom attendant, left-luggage officer, warehouseman and shoe repairer do not, in ordinary speech, 'supply' their customers. Lord Goff was further of the opinion that the particular offence in question was aimed at drug 'pushers'; the 20 defendant was not a 'pusher' and should have been charged with the lesser offence of 'unlawful possession'. If, he said, persons in the position of the defendant were to be convicted of 'possession with intent to supply', it was up to Parliament and not the courts to enlarge the definition of 'supply'.

(a) Line 15 of the source refers to extrinsic aids. Explain the meaning
of extrinsic aids and describe two examples. (12 marks + 3 marks)

(b) Using the source and your knowledge of the rules of statutory
interpretation, consider whether each of the following has
committed an offence by having 'a controlled drug in his possession,
whether lawfully or not, with the intent to supply it to another'
(lines 2–3).
  (i) Lucy has cannabis in her handbag, which she intends to smoke
  later in the day with her boyfriend Mike.
  (ii) Norris, a doctor, has taken controlled drugs from his patient
  Owen, an addict, and is planning to deliver these to the police.
  (iii) Paula is Quentin's mother. One day Quentin asks Paula to keep
  a sealed brown paper package for him while he goes out, and to
  give it back to him later. Unknown to Paula, the package
  contains cocaine. (15 marks)

(c) (i) Using the source and other cases, explain the literal rule.   (15 marks)
(ii) Discuss the advantages and disadvantages of using the
literal rule.   (12 marks + 3 marks)

■ ■ ■

A-grade answer

(a) Extrinsic means external and therefore extrinsic aids are ones outside the Act itself that a judge may use to help interpret words in the Act that are called into question in a case. They are different from intrinsic or internal aids, which are things that a judge can use to help with interpretation that are found in the Act itself, such as the title or schedules.

The extrinsic aid in the source is the *Shorter Oxford English Dictionary*. Lord Goff uses a dictionary to find the plain meaning of 'supply', the word in question in the case of *Maginnis*. One problem with using a dictionary is that the meaning of words can change over time, so a dictionary from the time of the Act would be best.

Another extrinsic aid is *Hansard*, which contains the reports of parliamentary debates. These reports tell the judge what was in the minds of the MPs at the time they were passing the Act. Lord Denning was reprimanded for using *Hansard* in *Davis* v *Johnson*, but its use is now allowed since the case of *Pepper* v *Hart*. This case said that it can only be used if the statement referred to was clear and has been addressed during the debate by the relevant minister.

> 🖉 This is a good answer and shows detailed understanding. It conforms with the requirements set (explain extrinsic aids and describe two examples). It makes useful reference back to the source, but builds on the source and uses cases. The contrast with intrinsic aids is also a useful inclusion.

(b) (i) Lucy would be guilty under the Act, whichever rules were used. As in the source, if the literal rule were used, the word 'supply' would cover the situation. The purpose of the Act was also to stop people like Lucy from passing on illegal drugs, so the mischief rule or the purpose rule would still find her guilty.

(ii) If the literal rule were used, then Norris would be found guilty as in the source. This seems to be an absurd result because Norris was only intending to be a good citizen and give the drugs to the police, so the judge might use the golden rule instead to avoid his conviction. It was not Parliament's intention to convict people like Norris but rather drug pushers, so if the mischief rule or the purposive approach were used then he would not be convicted.

(iii) This case is more difficult. It is like the examples that Lord Goff gives in the source and Paula should not really be convicted for supply unless she knew what was in the package. If the literal rule were used, she would be convicted under *Maginnis*, but another rule should be used to find her not guilty of supply.

> 🖉 The candidate gives very good and full answers to both (i) and (ii), applying the rules in turn and showing real understanding. For (iii) the candidate has spotted

the problem thrown up by the source and might have written a more detailed answer, possibly even referring to *Sweet* v *Parsley* and the general presumption of *mens rea*. Nevertheless, overall it is a good answer and the rules of statutory interpretation are clearly applied.

(c) (i) The literal rule is when a judge looks at the words of an Act and gives them their plain, ordinary literal meaning. As Lord Esher said in *R* v *City of London Court*, they must do this even if it would lead to an absurd result. The literal rule was developed by judges in the nineteenth century and was the main rule for most of the twentieth century too, but now, because of membership of the European Union, judges are more likely to use the purposive approach.

A major case showing how the literal rule could lead to an absurd result is *Fisher* v *Bell*. In this case the shopkeeper had flick-knives in his window and the Act said that a person should be convicted of the crime if he offered for sale an offensive weapon of which a flick-knife is one. In contract law, where goods are displayed it is an invitation to treat, not an offer. The judges applied the literal meaning and would not convict. This was absurd because it meant shopkeepers could not be convicted, so Parliament had to pass a new Act.

The literal rule can lead to injustice. This is what happened in *Berriman* v *London North Eastern Railway Company* where a man was killed while filling oil boxes on the railway line. His wife was unable to claim compensation because the Act only gave compensation for repairing and relaying, and the judges said that this did not include maintenance.

Another absurd case was *Whiteley* v *Chappell* where the defendant was allowed to get away with using someone else's vote because the other person had died and the Act said 'entitled to vote' and the court held that a dead person would not be entitled to vote.

Another case using the literal rule was *IRC* v *Hinchey*. Here, a man had not paid all his tax and the Act said that he should pay a fine of three times the amount owed. The judges used the literal rule and said that he had to pay three times what he originally owed and ignored the fact that he had paid some of it off already, so this was another absurd result.

(ii) The advantage of using the literal rule is that it recognises the separation of powers. Judges are not supposed to make law, Parliament is, so if there are any mistakes in an Act it is up to Parliament to change it and not the judges. This is also a disadvantage of the literal rule because Parliament may then have to pass another Act, which is what they did in *Fisher* v *Bell*. The literal rule is also advantageous in that it prevents judges from having too much power and, if the plain meaning is given rather than letting judges make up their own meaning, this prevents them from being too creative, which is what the mischief rule is criticised for. A disadvantage is that it cannot be used for European law because judges are supposed to use the purposive approach in this area. Another advantage of the literal rule is that it is said to produce consistency in the law if the plain meaning of words is given. However, words do not always have plain meanings and, if the judge uses a dictionary, dictionaries often give different meanings for the same word. Another advantage of using the literal rule is that it saves time because judges are less likely to use extrinsic aids. Obviously the rule as described by Lord Esher as above could be a disadvantage if using the rule is allowed to cause absurdities in the law. Another disadvantage of the literal rule is that it can lead to harsh or unjust results, as in *Berriman* above.

On the whole there are both advantages and disadvantages to using the literal rule, but there are probably more disadvantages and the purposive approach is probably a better rule to use now.

> ✏ The candidate has given a clear definition of the rule and even knows the implications of Lord Esher's statement on it. There is extensive use of case law, which is generally well explained. The candidate has engaged in a good discussion and not just added a list of advantages and disadvantages at the end but has taken care to thread some of them as comment next to the cases that have been used. Although it is quite limited in its scope, the candidate has also added a conclusion which lends weight to the discussion.

■ ■ ■

C-grade answer

(a) The extrinsic aid referred to in the source is the *Shorter Oxford English Dictionary*, although any type of dictionary might be used. In the source, the dictionary was used in order to find out the meaning of the word 'supply'.

Another extrinsic aid would be *Hansard*, the reports of parliamentary debates. This was allowed to be used after *Pepper* v *Hart,* providing that the statements to be looked at were clear and were made by the minister introducing the Act. *Hansard* is useful because it allows the judge to know what Parliament intended when it was passing the Act.

> ✏ The candidate forgot to explain the meaning of extrinsic aids, which means that full marks would not be available. Two extrinsic aids are identified, along with some reasonable explanation of what they are used for and some extra detail, so the candidate would still gain good marks for two thirds of the question.

(b) (i) Lucy would be guilty under the Act if the literal rule were used because the plain meaning of the word 'supply' includes Lucy giving some of the drugs to her boyfriend to smoke. This is what the Act was supposed to stop. If Lucy were only to smoke the cannabis herself and not give Mike any, then she could only be guilty of possession.

(ii) Norris would be guilty if the literal rule were used because the source says 'a person in unlawful possession of a controlled drug left with him for safekeeping by another person had the necessary intent to supply it to another (even though the supply was not being made from the provider's own resources) if his intention was to return it to the other person and for that other person's

question

purposes', which is the case here. Norris is intending to give the drugs to the police for their purposes, so he would be guilty under the literal rule. If the literal rule were used, then this would be unfair on Norris as he is only trying to do the right thing by giving the drugs to the police and he is trying to protect his patient, so it would produce an absurd result. The judge should use the golden rule when an absurd result happens with the literal rule like in *Adler* v *George*. The golden rule is to prevent the absurdity, so Norris would not then be guilty. The mischief rule could also be used because the mischief the Act was trying to cure was drug pushers and this would not include Norris, so he would not be guilty of the offence. The same thing applies with the purposive approach. The purpose of the section was to prevent drug pushers, so there is no need to use the Act against Norris in this way and he should not be convicted.

(iii) It would be unfair to convict Paula because she does not know what is in the brown paper package. As Lord Goff says, she is not supplying, she is just returning it.

✎ The candidate in (i) misses the point that there would be a conviction whatever rule applies, but answers appropriately on the literal rule. There is also a vague hint at the purposive approach in the second sentence, but the third sentence is not relevant. Answer (ii) is very long-winded, but all the points required to answer the question are included and all rules are correctly applied. The answer for (iii) is quite limited but hints at some understanding, even without mentioning the literal rule, and makes the connection with the source. If the candidate had applied better exam technique and remembered to apply all of the rules, he/she could have been awarded an A grade for this answer. The understanding was there; it just was not fully expressed.

(c) (i) The literal rule is where the words are given the ordinary literal meaning. The literal meaning could be found by looking in a dictionary, as happened in the source where the word 'supply' was looked up.

Maginnis was a case where the literal rule was used. The defendant was found guilty because the judges said that a person in unlawful possession of a controlled drug left with him for safekeeping by another person had the necessary intent to supply it to another if he intended to return it. Lord Goff says that this is not the meaning of supply in the Act, which is to convict drug pushers, so Maginnis should not have been convicted for supplying, showing that the literal rule can produce absurd results.

Another case using the literal rule is *Berriman*. This was where a man was killed while doing maintenance work on a railway. The Act held that the railway company would be liable if anybody were killed while repairing or relaying, but the judges said that maintenance was not the same as repairing or relaying, so the man's widow could not get compensation from the railway. This shows that the literal rule can cause injustice. Another case is *Fisher* v *Bell*.

(ii) The advantages of the literal rule are that it leaves the law making to Parliament, which is elected, rather than the judges, who are unelected, and it stops the judges from being too creative. Further, the ordinary meaning is given so there should not be any confusion. The disadvantages of the literal rule are that it can lead to absurdities and unjust results, and it may not give the answer that Parliament intended. It also means that people may be found guilty of crimes that they did not really commit, for example in *Maginnis*.

📝 The candidate uses a lot of information from the source, but there is also reasonable discussion of a case not in the source. A range of advantages and disadvantages are introduced in (ii), although these are not really presented as a discussion and there is no conclusion.

■ ■ ■

E-grade answer

(a) An extrinsic aid that could be used is *Hansard*. *Hansard* is the report of what goes on in debates in Parliament when an Act is being passed. The report is kept on a daily basis. *Hansard* has been allowed to be used since the case of *Pepper v Hart*. It could not be used before that. The case still gave restrictions on when it can be used, for example that it must be what the minister said in Parliament on the Act. Extrinsic means outside, and extrinsic aids are things that are outside the Act. *Hansard* is about the Act when it was being passed; it is not inside the Act itself.

📝 The candidate has given a good account of *Hansard*. There is also a reasonable explanation of what extrinsic aids are. However, the candidate has not followed the instruction to provide two examples and, surprisingly, has missed the one given in the source.

(b) (i) Lucy could be found guilty, whatever rule of statutory interpretation was used.

(ii) Norris could be found guilty using the literal rule, but this would be absurd because the doctor is not a drug pusher — he is only intending to give the drugs to the police, which is what he should do anyway. Perhaps the golden rule could be used because the literal rule would lead to an absurdity. If the mischief rule were used, then he would not be found guilty because Parliament was trying to punish drug pushers, not people handing over drugs to the police.

(iii) Paula would not be found guilty using the literal rule because she is not supplying drugs; she is only holding a package for her son. She would not be guilty using the mischief rule either because Parliament was trying to punish drug pushers, not innocent people like Paula.

📝 The answer to (i) is thin but accurate. The answer to (ii) gives good application of all of the rules, even though the purposive approach is not used. The candidate has clearly answered incorrectly on the literal rule in (iii) but is accurate on the mischief rule.

question

(c) (i) There are three rules of statutory interpretation: the literal rule, the golden rule and the mischief rule. The literal rule is used to find the meaning of a word. The literal rule is used by referring to a dictionary.

(ii) The disadvantage of the literal rule is that it leads to absurdities.

This is a very limited response. Some credit can be given for the recognition of the three rules and, although it is not explained, the link with dictionary meanings. There is also some limited AO2 credit for the one disadvantage recognised. This part of the answer is a long way from being a pass.

Overall, this is a typical E-grade response. The candidate gives quite good answers to (a) and (b), despite some errors or failing to do everything asked by the question. However, for part (c), which carries half the marks for the paper, there is only a very limited response.

Additional examiner comment

Go back to Question 1 and read the first two paragraphs in the 'Additional examiner comment'. Here you will find the advantages of source-based questions and some important points on preparing your answer in the exam.

In the source above there is lots of information that you can use to good effect. Below is an outline of what you can use from the source for each part of the question as well as other information not in the source but which the examiner would hope to see in a good script.

Part (a)
Information you can find in the source
In the fourth paragraph of the source there is a reference to extrinsic aids. There is also one example of an extrinsic aid, the *Shorter Oxford English Dictionary*, and some explanation of how and why it was used in the case of *Maginnis*, to find the plain meaning of the word 'supply'.

Extra information you should give in your answer
You should be able to work out from the example given that extrinsic aids are ones that are outside the Act itself. You should, in any case, provide a definition of that sort. You are also asked to explain the term 'extrinsic aids', so you should say why they are used, i.e. to help interpret words in dispute to find the intention of Parliament. You might also say that extrinsic aids provide specific understanding of words used in an Act that may not be found elsewhere.

You are asked to describe two extrinsic aids. You have been given one in the source and, if you use it well, you only need to search your memory for one other. There are many you could choose from: other similar Acts, past cases, leading textbooks, and the more controversial ones — *Hansard*, Royal Commission reports, Law Commission reports, even *travaux preparatoires* where EU law is involved. A brief explanation of how and why the aid is used is also needed. For example, *Hansard* would be useful to find out what happened in the debates as the bill passed through Parliament, but it can only be used subject to the rules laid down in *Pepper v Hart*.

Part (b)
Information you can find in the source
Application questions are all about using the information in the source and applying it to factual situations given in the questions, so you cannot really answer question (b) without using the source.

Here are a few points in the source to help you:
- the offence under s. 5(3) of the Misuse of Drugs Act 1971 in the first paragraph
- a simple definition of the literal rule at the beginning of the fourth paragraph
- the basic facts of Maginnis in the second paragraph and the way that the literal rule was applied in the third paragraph
- the problems Lord Goff identifies with the use of the literal rule in the fourth paragraph

Extra information you should give in your answer
Your task is to apply the above information to the individual questions, but here you also need to have an understanding of the golden rule, the mischief rule and the purposive approach.

For (i) you should spot that the literal meaning could lead to a conviction and that the purpose for which the Act was passed is satisfied because this is the type of situation Parliament was trying to prevent, so the mischief rule or the purposive approach would produce the same result. You could also say that because using the literal rule would not cause an absurd result, there is no need to apply the golden rule.

For (ii) you should be able to identify that using the literal rule would incur the possibility of injustice or absurdity and that the golden rule might be used to prevent this. You should also identify that using the mischief rule or the purposive approach would give a different result to the literal rule and should be preferred.

For (iii) you should be able to spot that this is the type of problem that Lord Goff identifies and is therefore more difficult. Using the literal rule would lead to a conviction which might cause injustice. Again, one of the other rules or approaches should be preferred. You might also see the relevance of *Sweet* v *Parsley* and the need to prove *mens rea* because the word 'supply' indicates an awareness of what has been handed over and some intention on the defendant's part.

Part (c)
Information you can find in the source
There is quite a lot of information in the fourth paragraph on the literal rule:
- the definition of the literal rule, giving the words their 'plain ordinary meaning'
- the reference to using dictionary meanings
- the difficulty that Lord Goff identifies in that the wrong meaning may be given and also that judges may have different views of what the plain meaning of a word is

Besides this, the case included in the source itself is an example of a literal rule case.

Extra information you should give in your answer
The most important additional information in (i) is extra cases for AO1 and in (ii) examples of advantages and disadvantages for AO2.

There are several cases you may know and use: *LNER* v *Berriman* (1946); *Whiteley* v *Chappell* (1868); *Fisher* v *Bell* (1960); *IRC* v *Hinchey* (1960); *Magor & St Mellons* v *Newport Corporation* (1950);

question

Cheesman v *DPP* (1990). You might also use golden rule cases such as *Re Sigsworth* (1935) or mischief cases such as *Smith* v *Hughes* (1960) to show up the disadvantages of the literal rule had it been used. You might also add that Lord Esher said in *R* v *City of London Court* (1892) that judges must apply the plain meaning even if it would lead to an absurd result.

For good AO2 marks you could identify the following advantages and disadvantages of the literal rule.

Advantages:
- it conforms to the separation of powers theory
- it prevents judges from making the law
- it prevents inconsistent meanings being given and is a simple rule to use

Disadvantages:
- it can lead to absurd results (*Hinchey*)
- it can lead to unjust results (*Berriman*)
- it can force Parliament to pass another Act (*Fisher* v *Bell*)
- it does not take account of changes in meanings over time or of technical meanings
- it presumes impossible levels of perfection in draftsmanship

European Union law

The role of the European Court of Justice (ECJ) is fundamental in ensuring legal enforcement of Community obligations and in ensuring uniform interpretations of EU law. It
has also been important in defining the principle of direct effect, although it was identified in *Marshall* v *Southampton and South West Hampshire Health Authority* (1986) that a
5 directive can only ever have vertical, not horizontal, direct effect.

Cases reach the ECJ either through direct actions, or through references on points of
Community law by national courts under Article 234. Article 234 creates a power, and
in some circumstances imposes a duty, to refer questions concerning the interpretation
of EU law to the ECJ. It plays a key role in ensuring the preservation of the Community
10 character of the law established by the treaty, and has the object of ensuring that in all
circumstances this law is the same in all states. The mandatory reference applies only
in a court where there can be no further appeal. Also, in order for there to be a duty to
refer, the question must be 'necessary'.

In *CILFIT* the ECJ held that there was no need to refer a question if it was not relevant,
15 if the answer to the question 'can in no way affect the outcome of the case' or where
there is an existing interpretation. English courts have interpreted this more liberally as
meaning 'reasonably necessary'.

(a) **Using the source and cases, explain the terms horizontal
direct effect and vertical direct effect (line 5).** (12 marks + 3 marks)

(b) **In each of the following situations consider whether the English
court would have either a duty or a power to refer a question to
the European Court of Justice under Article 234:**
  (i) **Ann has made a claim in an employment tribunal for equal
  pay. Clarification of a key point contained in a directive is
  likely to resolve the issue.**
  (ii) **A communications company has appealed a case concerning
  competition law to the House of Lords. The Court of Appeal
  has already accepted that an interpretation of EU law would
  decide the outcome of the case.**
  (iii) **A case on Sunday trading is being heard in a magistrates' court.
  An Article 234 reference in *Torfaen Borough Council* v *B & Q*
  (1990) has already identified that restrictions on Sunday trading
  are in breach of EU law.** (15 marks)

(c) (i) **Using the source and cases, explain the role of the ECJ.** (15 marks)
  (ii) **Discuss the ways in which it has been 'fundamental in
  ensuring legal enforcement of Community obligations and
  in ensuring uniform interpretations of EU law'.** (12 marks + 3 marks)

question

A-grade answer

(a) As the source says in the case of *Marshall* v *Southampton and South West Hampshire Health Authority,* a directive cannot have horizontal direct effect, only vertical direct effect. Mrs Marshall could only sue her employer because it was part of the state and so vertical direct effect could apply.

Vertical direct effect is when an individual can use European law to sue the state or an arm of the state where a directive has not been implemented. Regulations become law automatically in the UK and so they give both horizontal and vertical direct effect and an individual could use the regulation to sue either the state or another individual — whereas directives are given a time limit for the state to make them law so they cannot have horizontal direct effect. If they are not implemented within the time limit, they can still be enforced, but only through vertical direct effect.

Horizontal direct effect is when an individual can use European law to sue another individual.

✐ The distinction between horizontal and vertical direct effect is clearly shown, the source is used well and the example of direct effect of regulations also shows good understanding.

(b) (i) In Ann's case the employment tribunal would have the power to refer the case because under Article 234 any court has the power to refer and it is identified that a key point in the directive may decide the case.

(ii) The House of Lords has a duty to refer the company's case to the ECJ. This is because, as it says in the source, there is a mandatory referral in a situation 'when there is no further appeal' and there is no appeal from the House of Lords except to the ECJ.

(iii) This case could be referred to the ECJ because any court can refer and there is a breach of EU law. If the point of law is clear, then the magistrates' court might be able to decide the case itself.

✐ A clear understanding of discretionary and mandatory referrals is shown in (i) and (ii). Answer (iii) is wrong on the face of it, but there is some kind of idea that the *CILFIT* criteria might apply so that the court is bound to interpret the law itself.

(c) (i) The ECJ is the highest court in the hierarchy for all members of the European Union and all member states are bound to follow it. Britain became a member in 1972 by passing the EC Act and because of this it agreed to follow all EU law.

The ECJ has to ensure that all member states follow EU law and apply it properly. It has a number of roles. It hears Article 234 references from member states and gives interpretations of EU law that the courts are then bound to follow. This is so that there are 'uniform interpretations of EU law' in all the member states. The ECJ has developed a test in *CILFIT* to show when a court *can* refer and when it *has* to refer in a case. These are shown in the source.

Actions can also be taken in the ECJ against member states that breach EU law. The most important role of the ECJ is making sure that the member states follow EU law and do not make law against it. This can be seen in the *Factortame* case where the ECJ told the British government that the Merchant Shipping Act could not be used because it was in breach of EU law. The ECJ took the side of the Spanish fishing vessels in this case and made the British government follow EU law. This is known as supremacy of EU law.

(ii) As the source says, the ECJ has been important in defining direct effect. Direct effect is when individuals can sue using the EU law but if it is a directive, then only vertical direct effect can be used, as the source says was established in *Marshall*. If the individual is using a regulation, then both horizontal direct effect and vertical direct effect can be used. The *Tachographs* case is an example of this. If the ECJ had not developed direct effect, then individuals would not be able to enforce their rights under EU law.

The ECJ has also made member states pay compensation where they have not implemented a directive properly. In the case of *Francovich* the government was forced to pay compensation to some workers of a company that had gone insolvent as it had failed to implement a directive that would have meant the workers got compensated. This is called state liability. This is an example of the ECJ 'ensuring legal enforcement of Community obligations'. The *Factortame* case is another example. A further example is indirect effect, but this depends on the courts in the member states interpreting the law to include the unimplemented directive. The *Von Colson* case is an example of indirect effect.

The ECJ has a large role and courts being able to use the reference system means that there is a uniform application of the law throughout the member states.

📝 There is some good understanding here of what the question requires. Information from the source has been used effectively, but there is also much information on both supremacy and state liability which is extra to the hints given in the source. Cases have been used as asked for in the question. Some points could have been developed more, but overall the candidate has shown a broad understanding and answered well.

■ ■ ■

C-grade answer

(a) Vertical direct effect is when a member of the public wishes to challenge the state or an arm of the state in relation to a directive. For example, in the source in *Marshall* v *Southampton and South West Hampshire Health Authority* Mrs Marshall wanted to claim her rights to retire at the same age as a man under a directive. Because the health authority was run by the state, she was able to enforce the directive against it.

Horizontal direct effect, on the other hand, is when an individual wants to take action against another individual.

📝 The candidate shows some understanding of the difference between vertical and horizontal direct effect and of the relationship between state and non-state bodies, and has used some information from the source well, together with more detailed knowledge on the case of *Marshall*. However, the answer is limited to directives, and the full implications of direct effect are not developed.

(b) (i) The tribunal would have the power to refer the question to the ECJ because it involves EU law and clarification of a key point in a directive is likely to resolve the case.

(ii) The House of Lords would have to refer the case because it has already been decided that an interpretation of EU law would decide the case.

(iii) The court could refer because there is a breach of EU law.

📝 For (i) the candidate recognises the relevance of EU law and that the interpretation would resolve the case but does not say why the court could refer — the discretionary reference 'any court may'. For (ii) the candidate has done the same, omitting the obligation because the House of Lords is a court of last resort. For (iii) the candidate only spots the relevance of EU law but misses the fact that there is an existing interpretation binding the court. The candidate shows some general understanding but does not go far enough in justifying the answers with full knowledge of the procedures.

(c) (i) The ECJ has been fundamental in ensuring legal enforcement of Community obligations and in ensuring uniform interpretations of EU law. The ECJ is the highest court in Europe and in the UK, which is a member of the EU. The UK is bound by EU law, for instance on equal rights for men and women as in *Marshall* in the source.

The ECJ also hears references under Article 234 from member states. The ECJ gives interpretations of EU law, and the courts in the member states are then bound by those interpretations. All courts are able to refer if the reference is necessary. Some courts have to refer. This is known as a mandatory referral and is where there is no further appeal against the court. The case of *CILFIT* decided that there would not have to be a reference if it was not relevant, or if the answer to the question would not affect the outcome of the case or where there was already an interpretation. The Article 234 reference procedure is what ensures that EU law is applied in the same way in all the different states.

(ii) The ECJ plays a key role in ensuring the preservation of the Community character of the law established by the treaty. It does this by ensuring that all member states follow EU law.

The ECJ has defined direct effect where directives can only have vertical direct effect which is against the state. Horizontal direct effect is against an individual or business.

📝 The candidate has only really used information from the source. Nevertheless, the source has been well used and it is not merely copied. The candidate shows some good understanding in developing arguments and reaching conclusions from the information given.

E-grade answer

(a) Vertical direct effect is when the directive can be used against the state or an organ of the state. Horizontal direct effect is when the directive can be used against a private individual or a company.

📝 This is a limited answer in terms of its scope and development. The first sentence is correct but lacks explanation. The second sentence is plainly wrong. Directives can never be horizontally directly effective, although unfortunately this is an error made by many candidates.

(b) (i) The English court would have a power to refer a question to the European Court of Justice because it says that it is likely to resolve the case and there is no definite guidance.

(ii) The English court has a duty to refer the case. This is because the Court of Appeal has already identified that an interpretation of EU law would decide the case.

(iii) The English court would have a power to refer the question to the European Court of Justice. This is because an Article 234 reference in *Torfaen Borough Council* v *B & Q* (1990) has already identified that restrictions on Sunday trading are in breach of EU law. It may not be necessary for the English court to refer the question even though it has the power to do so.

📝 There is some recognition of the appropriate points in the answers here, but the candidate does not go far enough. For instance, there is no reasoning as to why each court can or must refer. The answer to (iii) shows some understanding of the point in the last sentence, but it lacks confidence or reasoning.

(c) (i) The main role of the European Court of Justice is ensuring legal enforcement of Community obligations and ensuring uniform interpretations of EU law. It has also been important in defining the principle of direct effect, although it was identified in *Marshall* v *Southampton and South West Hampshire Health Authority* (1986) that a directive can only ever have vertical, not horizontal, direct effect.

Another role is references on points of Community law by national courts under Article 234. Article 234 creates a power, and in some circumstances imposes a duty, to refer questions concerning the interpretation of EU law to the ECJ.

(ii) Another role is ensuring the preservation of the Community character of the law established by the treaty, with the object of ensuring that in all circumstances this law is the same in all states. It would be completely impractical if the law were different in all the individual member states.

Most of this has been copied from the source without much thought. There is nothing wrong with using the material in the source, but only limited credit can be given where it is merely copied. There is one good AO2 point right at the end, but overall the answer would not get a pass mark.

Overall, the answer to (a) is limited but with some accurate information. Answer (b) is reasonable, although it does not go far enough in explanation. Answer (c) shows a lack of confidence in the candidate, who for the most part copied chunks of the source and so would get only limited credit. Often E-grade answers are not as balanced in their marks as this would be.

Additional examiner comment

Go back to Question 1 and read the first two paragraphs in the 'Additional examiner comment'. Here you will find the advantages of source-based questions and some important points on preparing your answer in the exam.

In the source above there is lots of information that you can use to good effect. Below is an outline of what you can use from the source for each part of the question as well as other information not in the source but which the examiner would hope to see in a good script.

Part (a)
Information you can find in the source
In the first paragraph of the source there is reference to both horizontal and vertical direct effect. There is also the explanation that directives can never have horizontal direct effect but only vertical direct effect, and the example of *Marshall* for vertical direct effect.

Extra information you should give in your answer
Candidates often misinterpret the meaning of horizontal direct effect, although they usually have quite a clear idea of what vertical direct effect is. This can be clearly seen in the E-grade answer above.

You should provide a definition of both types of direct effect:
- Horizontal direct effect is the means by which citizens of member states can enforce measures of EU law against any other citizen or body.
- Vertical direct effect is one means of enforcing EU law against the state itself or against anything identified as an emanation or arm of the state according to the test in *Foster* v *British Gas* (1990).

You could identify that in the case of treaty Articles, because they are automatically law in the member state, they can be both horizontally and vertically directly effective, as in *Van Gend & Loos* or *Van Duyn*. The same point also applies to regulations for the same reason, and the *Tachographs* case is an example.

The point is made in the source that directives can only be enforced vertically against the state, but you might say why. This is because they do not automatically become law in member states but have to be implemented by them. You could also point out that in any case a directive cannot be vertically directly effective until the date for implementation is passed (*Ratti*) and the directive is not implemented at all or is only partly implemented.

Part (b)

Information you can find in the source

You are told quite a lot in the source. In the second paragraph you are given the reasons as to why references are made as well as an explanation of powers to refer (discretionary referral) and the duty to refer (mandatory referral). Besides this you have the *CILFIT* criteria in the third paragraph for when references should not be made. The question may also help you because in both (i) and (ii) you are told that an interpretation of EU law would resolve the cases and in (iii) because you have the example of one of the *CILFIT* criteria, with there being an existing interpretation in the *Torfaen BC* case.

Extra information you should give in your answer

Your task is to apply the above information to the individual questions.

For (i) you need to know that an employment tribunal would be classed as a court and therefore it will have the power to refer the case because under Article 234 any court has the power to refer. The question identifies that a key point in the directive may decide the case.

For (ii) you ought to be able to work out that the House of Lords has a duty to refer because the source tells you that there is a duty to refer 'when there is no further appeal' and you should be aware that there is no appeal from the House of Lords.

For (iii) you would know that the magistrates' court, being a court, has a power to refer. What you also need to remember is that in the source it tells you that there should be no unnecessary referral and there would be if there was an existing interpretation, and you have the example of *Torfaen* in the question itself.

Part (c)

Information you can find in the source

For (i) you are given some examples of the role of the ECJ in the second paragraph where the source refers to direct actions and references. Direct actions are those such as under Article 226 when actions are taken against member states for infringing their treaty obligations. You are given the reasons for making Article 234 references in the second paragraph.

For (ii), in the first paragraph you are given a major way in which the ECJ has ensured the enforcement of Community obligations with the creation of direct effect. For this you have been given the fact that directives only have vertical direct effect and have been given the case of *Marshall.* You also have the key way in which the ECJ ensures uniform interpretation of EU law, Article 234 references, for which there is a lot of detail you can use in the second and third paragraphs.

Extra information you should give in your answer

Most of the cases you know will have been Article 234 references, so you should be able to use them as examples. *Marshall* is a classic case.

It would help your AO1 mark if you used cases to illustrate the major developments made by the ECJ in ensuring enforcement of obligations:

question

- The doctrine of supremacy of EU law over that of member states — you could use *Van Gend & Loos* v *The Netherlands* (**1963**); *Simmenthal* (**1978**); *Costa* v *ENEL* (**1964**); or, best of all, *Factortame* (**1990**).
- For direct effect you could use *Van Gend & Loos* again, and on vertical direct effect *Marshall* (**1986**) and *Foster* v *British Gas* (**1990**) would be good for explaining what is meant by an 'arm of the state'. You might also use *Duke* v *GEC Reliance Ltd* (**1988**) to show the potential unfairness when an individual cannot sue another individual on a directive.
- You could explain the principle of indirect effect, that the national court interprets national law so as to incorporate the directive. Here the *Von Colson* (**1984**) case or *Marleasing* (**1992**) are relevant.
- You could also explain state liability — if the state has caused a person loss by its failure to implement EU law, then it must compensate that person. It would be good to include the conditions in *Francovich* (**1991**) and the changes to them made in the *Brasserie du Pecheur/Factortame (No 2)* (**1996**) case.

PHILIP ALLAN
UPDATES